THE DESERT

THE DESERT

AN ANTHOLOGY FOR LENT

JOHN MOSES
Dean of St. Paul's Cathedral

MOREHOUSE PUBLISHING

First American edition published by

Morehouse Publishing
P.O. Box 1321
Harrisburg, PA 17105
Morehouse Publishing is a division of The Morehouse Group.

Library of Congress Cataloging-in-Publication Data

Moses, John.
    The desert : an anthology for Lent / John Moses.
      p. cm.
    Originally published: Norwich, England : Canterbury Press, 1997.
    Includes bibliographical references.
    ISBN: 978-0-8192-1728-8
    1. Lent—Meditations. 2. Holy Week—Meditations. I. Title.
BV85.M634 1998
242' .34—dc21
                                                   97-37678
                                                    CIP

Second Printing, 2001

Printed in the United States of America

'Then the desert held me:
would that it had never
let me go!'

St Jerome

Contents

Contents

ACKNOWLEDGEMENTS

I am glad to acknowledge the permission that has been granted to quote directly from a large number of published works in the compilation of the Anthology. Every attempt has been made to secure permission to use copyright material, and all such material is fully acknowledged in the Notes at the end of the book.

I am glad also to acknowledge the unfailing support that has been provided by Mr Kenneth Baker, of the Canterbury Press Norwich, with whom it has been so helpful to liaise from the beginning in the writing and publication of this book.

But nothing could have been submitted to the publisher without the wholehearted support of Mrs Anita Butt who, in the midst of a busy professional life, has worked tirelessly and enthusiastically in the typing and preparation of the manuscript for publication.

Preface

THE renewal of the church requires a continuing exploration of its traditions of faith and prayer. These traditions must be true to scripture and to our experience of living in the world. They will speak of the absolute priority of God. Their authenticity will be judged by the degree to which they are honest, critical, pragmatic, robust, and life-affirming.

It is one of the intriguing paradoxes of the contemporary church that there should be a significant revival of interest in the desert tradition of spirituality. The story of the desert is associated in the minds of many people with the Desert Fathers of the fourth and fifth centuries; but the tradition has its roots in the scriptures and finds repeated expression in the individual journeys of large numbers of people. The fascination of the desert lies in the fact that it has nothing to offer. It speaks of the abandonment of *everything* in favour of *nothing*; or, to be more accurate, of the abandonment of everything in favour of God – *and God alone*.

The desert encapsulates an ideal which has found expression down the centuries in the life of the church. This ideal has been explored in our own day by travellers and writers, by theologians and mystics. But the desert is not merely a place. It is a *type* of Christian experience. The emptiness and the silence of the desert stand as symbols of the desolation, the isolation, to which some are condemned at periods of their life.

It is an awareness of these things that has led to the preparation of this book and the compilation of an anthology of desert spirituality for personal use during Lent. It has seemed right to sketch in fairly general terms something of the story and the spirituality and the literature of the desert. It is hoped that these brief chapters will provide a helpful background to the anthology. But it is the anthology that constitutes the substance of the book.

Lent is the spring-time of the church's year. It is the season of renewal. Any reading of the spirituality of the desert suggests five great themes – solitude, testing, self-emptying, encounter, and transfiguration. It is these themes which provide the framework within which numerous quotations from the desert tradition of faith and prayer are set. Every attempt has been made to draw upon a wide range of Christian literature, but it ought not to pass unnoticed that well over one half of all quotations are taken from writers of the twentieth century.

Readers of this book will obviously use it in their own ways. There are certain things that might be said, however, to those who want to take the anthology as a basis for daily reflection and prayer during Lent. Try to be alone. Do not be in a hurry. Take one day at a time. Read each saying quietly. Let the words speak to you. Be willing to stay with one saying and to read it again and again. Allow the words to confront you, to search and test you.

There is one other consideration which suggests that the publication of an anthology of desert spirituality might well be timely. There is a good deal of concern on every side that the church – all churches – might find effective ways of communicating the Gospel to a generation which seems to be increasingly indifferent. There are deep-seated changes within the *mores* of our developed societies in the western world, and the church appears all too often to have lost its foothold. But a church that understands the tradition of the desert will know what it means to hold the faith in obscurity and in silence, living with its brokenness and its incompleteness, watching and waiting.

London   JOHN MOSES

THE STORY
OF THE DESERT

THERE has been a revival of interest throughout much of this century in the story and the spirituality of the desert. The story of the desert is associated in the minds of many people with the Desert Fathers of the fourth and fifth centuries; but the desert tradition has its origin for Christian people in the scriptures and not merely in the story of the church.

The long years of the Exodus were a period of testing and discovery. It was in the wilderness that the children of Israel found their identity as a people, their God, their law, their vocation. Nothing could ever be the same again. It was the defining moment in the light of which the whole of their subsequent history must be interpreted.

The flight of the prophet Elijah and the refuge that he found in the wilderness ensured the continuing vitality of the desert tradition. It was a tradition – an experience – that must encompass something of his passionate and single-minded search for God, the uncompromising quality of his obedience, the prophetic call to repentance, the word of judgement.

It was the identification of the desert experience with the prophetic word which was presented so dramatically in the person and the teaching of John the Baptist. But his ministry did not merely serve as a fulfilment of scripture. It pointed forward to the One who would baptise with the Holy Spirit and with fire. It spoke, therefore, of revelation and renewal in the power of God.

The meaning of all these things found their full expression in the person of Jesus. The temptations in the wilderness were for Him a period of testing and discovery. The long nights of prayer alone on the hillside were the bed-rock of His passionate and single-minded search for God, the uncompromising quality of His obedience. The agony of the garden, the torment of self-abandonment, led inexorably to the sacrifice of the cross, and to the transformation of God's people by His decisive act of redemption and renewal.

There is a solitude of the spirit which has found expression in all ages, in all parts of the world, and in men and women of all races and religious faiths. The desert tradition has been a continuing theme throughout Israel's long history. It was embodied – actually lived out and worked through – in the life and ministry of Jesus. But the desert has never been an end in itself. To be alone in the desert is to be alone with God. The invitation of the desert is the call to love God – *absolutely.*

Palestine drew Christian people from an early period from all parts of the Mediterranean world who chose to live in great solitude and simplicity. Hermits established themselves in the Egyptian desert as early as the third century. The great monastic centres – the places associated with the Desert Fathers of the fourth and fifth centuries – were to be found in Egypt and Syria and Palestine.

These early desert communities fell into three broad categories. There were the men who became the disciples of St Antony[1] in Lower Egypt. He provided a basic rule, but his followers lived lives of great solitude and asceticism, far removed from the corporate life associated with the developed monasticism of later centuries.

There were at a similar time in Upper Egypt communities which derived their inspiration from St Pachomius.[2] It is reckoned that by the time of his death there were as many as nine monasteries for men and two for women, living under a simple rule which became the rule for the monastic foundations of St Basil later in the fourth century.

But there were also small groups of men and women, settled in large measure in the Nitrian desert to the west of the mouths of the Nile, known as *laura* or *skete*. These had been established by St Ammon[3] in Nitria and St Macarius[4] in Scetis. The members of these communities settled in close proximity to a spiritual father, but they lived their separate lives for much of the time, coming together at the weekend to share the eucharist.

Desert monasticism in these early centuries attracted large numbers of people. Some undoubtedly found a refuge in the desert at times of persecution. Others by contrast found the peace that followed upon these periodic outbursts of

persecution to be too comfortable. They sought in the solitude and the rigours of the desert something that might serve
as a substitute for martyrdom. Some sought an escape from
the burdens of taxation or the demands of military service.
But there were others for whom the migration to the desert
was a conscious turning away from a church that had
become established in public esteem. They rejected any
accommodation between the church and the world that was
too facile, too complaisant.

The idea of the world as a foreign country had gone deep
into the consciousness of the early church. The desert encap-
sulated an ideal which would continue to find expression
down the centuries in the life of the church. The movement to
the desert was so much more than a flight from a civilization
in decline. It represented in its solitude and its simplicity the
absolute priority of the spiritual life. It was the abandonment
of *everything* in favour of *nothing* which was the bed-rock of
the desert tradition and of the religious life. Or rather: it was
the abandonment of everything in favour of God – *and God
alone* – which gave to the desert experience its compulsion
and its continuing appeal.

A succession of travellers – Basil the Great,[5] Rufinus,[6]
Melania,[7] Jerome,[8] Palladius,[9] John Cassian[10] – have left
accounts of what they found in the desert. Their writings
have provided the primary sources for the sayings of the
Desert Fathers, but they have also given us a picture of life in
the desert.

The pattern of life varied greatly from place to place. The
character of what was attempted by the followers of St
Antony was captured in an idealised account by St
Athanasius,[11] who wrote of 'the cells ... in the mountains,
like tabernacles, filled with holy bands who sang psalms,
loved readings, fasted, prayed, rejoiced in the hope of things
to come, laboured with alms-giving, and preserved love and
harmony with one another'.[12]

The more developed forms of community life in Upper
Egypt and in the Nitrian desert produced their own significant variations, but the inhospitable nature of the desert

provided the backcloth to lives of poverty and great simplicity. There was inevitably a daily struggle to survive: the perennial need for water; the most primitive forms of agriculture; the repetitive labour of making baskets and rush mats. There is ample evidence of isolation, boredom, eccentricity, frustration, depression, spiritual warfare. But the vocation of a life that was to be lived for God remained and found expression in the routine of devotion, in patterns of spiritual oversight, in traditions of charity and hospitality.

It is the sayings of the Desert Fathers that provide the most significant insights into the pattern of religious life in the desert – its routine, its rhythm, its underlying purpose, its temptations. These sayings have been properly described as 'a series of disconnected snap-shots'.[13] They were invariably addressed to individuals in response to specific questions. They were not concerned to express some abstract principle which might have a universal application. It was their practical wisdom, their innate common sense, that gave them their spiritual authority. The sayings were undoubtedly repeated, passing from person to person, from place to place. They have been made available in recent generations in a succession of anthologies. Their meaning for our understanding of the desert story lies in their repeated emphasis upon silence, solitude, penitence, prayer, perseverance, obedience.

The desert drew men and women in large numbers. It was reported by travellers at the end of the fourth century that the population of the desert equalled that of the towns.[14] And yet there is repeated reference to the silence which is clearly so much more than the silence of the physical desert. It was as though the immensity of the desert and the totality of the commitment of those who made their way there met and found a shared and characteristic expression in 'a mighty silence and a great quiet among them'.[15]

The Desert Fathers of these early centuries have been seen in retrospect as charismatic figures, bearers of the Spirit, authentic voices of truth. The story and the spirituality of the desert have found expression down the centuries in a great variety of ways; but the desert tradition, which was embodied by the Desert Fathers, unquestionably became the inspiration of Christian monasticism.

Religious communities established themselves at an early stage in Palestine, in Asia Minor, along the coast of North Africa, and then – penetrating farther afield – in Greece, in Italy, in Spain and in Gaul. By the sixth century monasticism had established itself as a vital ingredient within the life and ascetical tradition of the church.

The rule of St Benedict[16] provided the pattern for monasticism in the western church, but behind the developed forms of monasticism in later centuries lay the primary emphasis upon the call to holiness. The solitary life of the Desert Fathers had been an affirmation of a life that is lived alone with God. The corporate life of the medieval communities gave public expression to the priorities of the desert tradition – prayer, study, manual labour. The monasteries of medieval Europe made a massive contribution to agriculture, architecture, scholarship, government, and community life; but their starting point was the consecration of a life that is lived with and for God.

The desert ideal – abandoning *everything* in favour of *nothing* – became the perennial point of reference in the life of the church as later generations sought to rediscover an earlier tradition. The eleventh and twelfth centuries witnessed the foundation of new orders or communities where silence, simplicity and solitude were the building blocks of a renewed monasticism.

A community of Benedictine hermits was founded by St Romauld[17] at Camaldoli in Italy in the late tenth century which emphasised the solitary character of the religious life. The Carthusian Order, which was established by St Bruno[18] in the eleventh century, although it had no special rule at the beginning, demanded silence, solitude and contemplation. The Cistercian Order, associated with St Bernard of Clairvaux[19] in the twelfth century, was characterised by the building of its houses in remote places and by the simplicity and strictness of its rule. The Carmelite Order, founded in Palestine in the middle years of the twelfth century, claimed continuity with the hermits settled on Mount Carmel in earlier times, and ordered its common life around the disciplines of solitude, absolute poverty, and extreme asceticism.

In the eastern church, there was from the early ninth century a revival of the solitary life centred upon Mount Athos. It is a way of life that has survived, albeit in greatly diminished numbers in recent times; and the physical characteristics of the promontory have ensured that those who choose this vocation might have a continuing place within the monasticism of the mountain. But the life that is hid with Christ in God[20] will express itself in many ways. The isolation of the desert place has always taken a variety of forms. In Russia in the fourteenth century it was the impenetrable forests that became associated with spiritual exploration and spiritual wisdom.

In England, by contrast, in the later middle ages it was the hermit cell or anchorage, often located in close proximity to a religious house, that spoke most powerfully of the life of total consecration. This form of religious obedience has been associated in English piety with Julian of Norwich[21] for whom the cell became a desert place – 'a desert that spoke to her in absolutes, a desert that stripped away the conditional, the passing and the transient. In the clear light of the desert she saw God and the soul'.[22]

There is evidence of a desire in the thirteenth and fourteenth centuries in western Europe to return to the simplicity of an evangelical Christianity. This found its most enduring expression in the Franciscan deal, embracing holy poverty, a true love of nature, missionary work, and brotherly and sisterly love.

But religious communities – like all churches and all traditions of faith – can lose their first love. The continuing need for reformation and renewal demands that the desert ideal must be rediscovered and re-interpreted in successive generations. Thomas Merton's interpretation of the work of Paul Giustiniani, who revived the hermit community at Camaldoli early in the sixteenth century, was that he sought 'to re-kindle the ancient fire that (was) burning low in an age that (had) no love for asceticism, for contemplation, or for solitude'.[23] That has been the abiding challenge.

The desert tradition had entered the bloodstream of the Christian church, and this tradition – this ideal – had been carried for over a thousand years by monasticism. The tradition required solitude and space. 'The desert, the mountain top, the frozen regions, the wild woods: all testify to the same experience of solitude and space. Spiritual maturity, like physical maturity, demands space, vastness, wildness.'[24] But the experience has never been confined to monasticism, and the desert experience remains an inescapable part of the journey of the soul towards God.

It is this aspect of personal discipleship that is conveyed in the writings of St John of the Cross.[25] His poetry and his spiritual treatises, mystical and contemplative in character, speak of the interior life of the soul and its engagement with God in love. But the images that he employs speak – like the desert – of privation, of negation, of pain, of darkness, of the night. It is in the experience of nothingness that the soul is drawn by love and responds in love. It is in the darkness of the night that the soul learns to rest in faith on God alone.

St John of the Cross has been associated with the reform of monasticism that was inspired by the counter-reformation. The centuries that followed were to see the growth of new orders, but his exposition of the spiritual life has endured as an authentic interpretation of the desert tradition. It is in the light of his understanding of the soul's encounter with God that the desert has become in more recent times a symbol – and far more than a symbol – for Charles de Foucauld.[26]

Charles de Foucauld had been advised at an early stage by his spiritual director to 'bury (himself) with our Lord, lost, unknown'.[27] His search for solitude took him to Nazareth, to Beni-Abbès, to the Hoggar Mountains, and finally to Tamanrasset. He has become known as the hermit of the Sahara, and his desire was to establish a new kind of religious order which would be characterised by a devotion to the blessed sacrament; by a life of identification with the poorest of God's people; and by giving simple hospitality to all who came, regardless of their faith or disposition.

Charles de Foucauld was emphatic that 'I am a *monk* and not a missionary, made for silence and not for speech'.[28] Long hours were spent in prayer, in manual work, in study, in translation, and in correspondence. The desert was to be for him a place of solitude, of hiddenness, where he could encounter God and express in simple ways a brotherly and universal charity.[29] It was, however, the pattern of total self-dispossession which became the inspiration of those who followed in his rediscovery of the desert tradition.

Charles de Foucauld's life of prayer and poverty has led since his death to the foundation of various communities – the Little Sisters of the Sacred Heart, the Little Brothers of Jesus, the Little Sisters of Jesus, and the Little Brothers and Sisters of the Gospel. They bear powerful testimony to the truth of the gospel saying that only the grain of wheat that falls into the ground and dies can bear a rich harvest.[30]

Some of these communities found their original vision in the *physical* desert with a special emphasis upon prayer, manual work, and the evangelisation of the poor. But there has been a significant change of direction in recent years, and the Little Brothers and Sisters have often made their homes in the *spiritual* desert that is to be found in some of the large urban centres throughout the world. These communities, which are often small in size, have become very numerous. They have held tenaciously to de Foucauld's vocation of 'living, rather than preaching, the presence of Christ in the world'.[31] It is undoubtedly the case that their life is more or less hidden from the world. It is inseparable in so many respects from that of their neighbours; but the life of prayer and devotion finds practical expression in their availability and hospitality to others.

It is the search for God – and God alone – which lies at the heart of the desert story. The more rigorous forms of monasticism have been the primary vehicle by which the desert tradition and the desert ideal have been expressed. But the physical desert has become a symbol of the experience of

God-forsakenness, of emptiness, of abandonment, of nothingness. The desert in this sense of the word is not a place
that people seek but an experience which surrounds them
and to which they find themselves condemned.

Something of the torment of this kind of desert experience
is inevitably expressed by poets and writers. T.S. Eliot, writing in the aftermath of the First World War, captures in *The
Waste Land* the sense of futility that is felt by a generation as
he reflects on 'the agony in stony places'.[32] Thomas Merton,
making connections between theology and life, tells of the
necessity to go down into nothingness if we are to receive
God's gift of hope.[33] Alexander Solzhenitsyn, drawing upon
his bitter experiences of the labour camps of Soviet Russia,
discerns a place 'beyond despair', where those who endure
the desolation of the spirit discover that God might yet be
found.[34] R.S. Thomas explores constantly throughout his
poetry in his honest, sombre way the perennial experience of
the presence and the absence of God, of the apparent emptiness of prayer.[35]

It is this far broader understanding of the desert which has
to be acknowledged before any account of the desert story
can be concluded. There is here – at least in our contemporary world – a state of mind, a way of being, through
which many will pass. It is in the wastelands of our experience that many are called to enter the darkness of our world
and find something of the truth of our condition. It is an
experience that takes many forms: the disappointments and
frustrations of human relationships; the grievous wounds
that men and women inflict upon one another; the capacity
for self-deception, self-destruction; the loss of confidence, of
faith, of vitality; the emptiness – the appalling emptiness –
of life; the inescapable facts of pain, of permanent disability,
of death.

These are some of the deserts of mind and spirit through
which men and women are required to travel. These are some
of the innumerable descents into nothingness that are lived
out every day. These deserts can, indeed, be places of torment
and despair; but they hold out the possibility of encounter
and renewal.

The desert is a place of truth. The experiences of the desert expose our weaknesses, search us out, test us. The desert can be 'the feeling of inner emptiness that comes from being cut off from the divine presence',[36] but it can also be the place of discovery. The need for solitude, which is so rarely achieved, can point towards the inner hermitage, which is the meeting ground of God with all who learn to rest in faith alone. The promise remains that the desert shall rejoice and blossom, that waters shall break forth in the wilderness, that the burning sand shall become a pool, and the thirsty ground springs of water.[37] The desert encapsulates an ideal which has found expression down the centuries in the life of the church – in the Egyptian desert; in the ordered life of the monastery; in the hermit cell; in the Russian forest; in the writings of mystics and poets; in the vocation of Charles de Foucauld and of the Little Brothers and Sisters of Jesus; in the torments of the human condition. It speaks of the hidden life, of endurance, of testing, of simplicity, of self-abandonment, of the silent prayer of the spirit. It bears witness to the absolute priority of God.

THE SPIRITUALITY
OF THE DESERT

THE story and the spirituality of the desert can never be entirely disentangled from each other. The men and women who have shaped the desert story may appear to be far removed from contemporary life as it is known throughout much of the world. Their writings speak of a way of responding to the gospel which is necessarily beyond the reach of all who are properly caught up in the preoccupations of life. Occasional glimpses of silence, of solitude, are often the only things that can provide some insight for many people into the life of the mystic, the hermit. But within the story of the desert there are aspirations and experiences which constitute the raw material of discipleship. The story does not merely tell of an impossible ideal which some are called to live out to an extraordinary degree. It speaks also of patterns of obedience which all are called to discover and make their own.

There has been a desire in recent decades to rediscover the spirituality of the desert. The fascination – even, perhaps, the compulsion – of the desert lies for many in the fact that it has nothing to offer. It stands, therefore, in sharp contrast to the secularity of modern life with its emphasis upon self-expression, self-fulfilment.

The desert affords no hiding place, no refuge. It is a place of desolation and liberation. One modern traveller speaks of the desert as an environment which humbles and exalts. Its immensity reduces 'our tiny, struggling world to insignificance'; and yet it sets a person free 'to think more profoundly ... to examine ... motivations, aims and objects in a new and surprisingly fresh light'.[1]

But the desert is not merely a place. It is a *type* of Christian experience. The vast emptiness and silence of the desert stand as symbols of the desolation, the isolation, to which some are condemned at periods of their life as an inescapable part of their journey. The desert as both place and experience becomes associated, therefore, with journeying; with testing; with seeking another country, a promised land.

The desert tradition speaks of the absolute priority of God. The desert is a place of truth, where men and women can find the truth about God and the truth about themselves. The immensity of the desert removes the pretensions of life. The barrenness of the desert prepares the way for the things that can only be accomplished by God. 'Living in the desert does not mean living without people, but living with God and for God.'[2]

The desert is no respecter of persons. It represents a day-by-day struggle to survive. It provides its own predicaments and temptations – isolation, boredom, an inflamed imagination, self-deception, frustration, depression. It involves a confrontation with the devils – the evil – within ourselves. And yet those who can face the truth of their condition become for others signs of hope. It is not the least of their achievements that 'they are broken, incomplete ... with their raw edges reaching always towards the heavens'.[3]

The desert takes us to the boundaries of human existence, of human experience. The physical austerities that are traditionally associated with the physical desert were designed to set men and women free so that they might see God. 'Fasting, virginity, labour, the reading and recitation of Holy Scripture, vigils, meditation, and even prayer itself, were looked upon simply as ways of arriving at a perfect life.'[4]

These disciplines are never seen as ends in themselves. What is required is dependence upon God, humility of heart, seriousness of purpose, tenacity of spirit. What is sought is an imitation of Christ in His poverty and self-abandonment. 'The desert does not allow any compromise.'[5]

There is, nonetheless, in the desert experience a pain that remains unseen and unregarded. The call to silence and prayer is renewed by the discipline of sacred learning and strengthened by the rigours of a thorough-going asceticism. But the life that is hid with Christ in God[6] must all too often bear in silence the aridity, the darkness, the desolation.

Asceticism is no substitute for discretion. Those who travel in the desert must be able to find their path. There is an urgent need for guidance, for spiritual direction. The sayings of the Desert Fathers display a profound common-sense, a practical wisdom. St Antony was emphatic that discretion is 'the mother, the guardian, the moderator of all virtues'.[7] To lack discretion is to run the serious risk of falling away from God. The wisdom of the desert has a timeless quality. It is primitive, pragmatic, self-effacing, and realistic.

All that might be said about the spirituality of the desert can be properly brought together within five great themes. They are *solitude, testing, self-emptying, encounter*, and *transfiguration*. These themes find expression throughout the story of the desert. They are inseparable from the physical desert. They are fundamental to the spiritual desert. They encapsulate in the hard realities of daily life all that has been said about journeying, testing, seeking. The desert is a place of discovery, of renewal. It is the place chosen by God where – at least for some – the divine drama of death and resurrection must be experienced and accomplished.

The *solitude* must never be confused with loneliness or isolation. Indeed, it does not necessarily imply an abandonment of the world. The invitation to go into one's room and shut the door and pray to the Father who is in secret[8] speaks of the solitude, the hiddenness, of the spirituality of the desert. But the solitary place, the inner hermitage, is the arena for engagement and encounter.

The solitude of the desert tells, therefore, of the necessity of waiting upon God. Patience, attentiveness, learning to be unhurried, waiting in silence, perseverance: these are not the least of the desert virtues. The teaching of the early Desert Fathers remains: 'Go and sit in thy cell, and thy cell shall teach thee all things'.[9]

What is being attempted is nothing less than a participation in the solitude and silence of God. The invitation is to seek and find God within ourselves. 'Find a place in your heart, and speak there with the Lord. It is the Lord's reception-room. Every one who meets the Lord meets Him there; He has fixed no other place for meeting souls.'[10] It is only in the deepest silence within ourselves that God's word can be heard.

Solitude and silence belong together. But the solitude that is achieved will soon be inhabited by those whom we bring with us. 'Solitude and silence are the context within which prayer is practised.'[11] It is in silence that we discover the empathy of prayer, entering into the joys and sorrows of others, experiencing our solidarity with those whom we hold before God. Solitude and silence serve to unite. 'The more we are alone with God the more we are united with one another.'[12]

The desert is a place of truth, and that implies that it is invariably experienced as a place of *testing*. The desert exposes our vulnerabilities. It brings to the surface the fears that are buried deep within ourselves. It can take us to the edge of all that we understand by normality, by sanity. The desert has been called 'the country of madness'.[13]

The desert tests in many ways. It will be for some a place of fantasy, of self-deception, 'the land of mirage'.[14] The desert offers no escape to those who are tested in this way. On the contrary, the true desert, the true wilderness of the spirit, demands confrontation. This will invariably involve a coming to terms with the truth about ourselves, confronting the demons within. There is always the need 'to take a closer look at the things and people one would rather not see, to face situations one would rather avoid, to avoid questions one would rather forget'.[15]

The desert speaks, therefore, of the idea of Christian discipleship as a life of constant warfare. Endurance, tenacity, forbearance, courage: these are the qualities that the desert requires of those who are to survive. The idea persists that the soul is brought to maturity only through testing. 'The desert is pure and purifies'.[16] The desert is both a journey into ourselves and a journey into God. The struggles that are associated with a spirituality of the desert are to be fought on several fronts. The prayer is not 'that the struggle be taken away ... but ... "Lord, give me strength to get through the fight" '.[17]

The spirituality of the desert challenges the prevailing assumption that life can only be lived through self-realisation and self-fulfilment. Such words, such attitudes, assume that we have the confidence to make life our own. They do not necessarily take account of our capacity for self-destruction, of the disorderliness of life, of the fragmentation of our private and our public worlds, of the innumerable griefs and torments that call into question everything that matters.

The desert speaks of *self-emptying*, of self-abandonment. It relates, therefore, to the central mystery of death and resurrection. It is the prayer of Gethsemane, 'Father, if it be possible let this cup pass from me; nevertheless, not as I will, but as thou wilt'.[18] It is the prayer of the hermit and the mystic, 'I want to give God everything'.[19]

Such a response appears to be far beyond the reach of many who hear the call to discipleship. It seems to represent an impossible ideal. We dare not aspire to it. It is, therefore, helpful to be reminded that what lies at the heart of this self-emptying is nothing more and nothing less than the will to love. But love must find a practical expression. The challenge to spend our lives in love of our neighbour[20] requires the right kind of self-confidence, an appropriate self-love, a humility, a freedom of the spirit. It demands above everything else an awareness of our dependence upon God.

There is a robust, worldly, life-affirming quality about the self-emptying of desert spirituality. The lines of demarcation between self-affirmation and self-abandonment are not necessarily so clearly drawn as these words might initially suggest. There are many who will find reassurance in the injunction, 'Act as though everything depended upon you. But pray as though everything depended upon God'.[21]

There is nothing in the spirituality of the desert that detaches us from life in any sense that matters. The desert is the place of *encounter*. The insight of the desert tradition that 'you are never less alone than when you are alone'[22] serves to remind that solitude, testing and self-emptying can only give way to a glorious and gracious discovery of God, of our Lord, of other people, and of ourselves.

But these encounters can only occur when there is an openness of mind, a generosity of spirit, which enable us to find our life and our being in relation to others. The judgement of the Desert Fathers is unanimous that 'Charity, not silence, is the purpose of the spiritual life'.[23] The character and the quality of all that is meant by the encounters of the desert are conveyed by the experience of early travellers in the Egyptian desert. 'What can I say that would do justice to their humanity, their courtesy, and their love ... Nowhere have I seen love flourish so greatly, nowhere such quick compassion, such eager hospitality.'[24]

St Antony's insistence that 'our life and our death are with our neighbour'[25] takes us far beyond traditions of hospitality. It points unequivocally towards a solidarity with people in their need. Charles de Foucauld, whose life has become the inspiration of the Little Brothers and the Little Sisters of Jesus, exhibited in all his dealings with people in the Sahara the gentleness, the deference, the graciousness, the courtesy that properly belong to the spirituality of the desert. But his innate regard for others was increasingly informed by what he found in the gospels as he reflected upon 'the respect with which Christ ... treated every human being: the woman taken in adultery; the woman who touched his garment in the crowd; the Samaritan woman at the well; Zacchaeus in the sycamore tree; the dying thief'.[26]

The desert becomes for many people 'an essential dimension of life'.[27] The spirituality of the desert can never be confined to the enlightenment or sense of liberation that might be given to an individual in the course of his or her own personal journey. The encounters of the desert require us to enter the 'disturbed solitude' of our daily lives,[28] and to find a place alongside 'the world and the world's misery'.[29] There is a universal condition of despair and hope, of judgement and promise. The desert invites us to encounter this world – to enter this world – with understanding, with empathy, with commitment, with passion.

There is, however, the promise that, 'If you are generous, little by little, you will see the divine world emerging from the shadows'.[30] *Transfiguration* is what happens when 'God's totality and man's nothingness'[31] engage with one another. The desert is never an end in itself. It is a time of preparation, of testing, of transition. The long years of the exodus lead from slavery to freedom.

The disciplines of prayer and study and fasting have always counted for much in the desert tradition. These ascetical disciplines have been concerned from the beginning to bring under control the appetites of the flesh and to focus the mind upon the things of God. But there lies beyond all these spiritual disciplines the vision of a life that is set free and restored and renewed. 'The glory of God is a man or a woman who is truly alive.'[32]

It is one of the more self-evident paradoxes of grace that only 'those who have nothing can accept everything';[33] but *everything* in this context is nothing less than the totality of God. The desert brings us back again to the divine mystery of death and resurrection, of life and death and life. The desert speaks of a descent into nothingness; but it is only there – in the depths, in the darkness – that we are able to receive the gift of hope, the promise of life. The desert is presented time and again in the literature of the church as the place of the cross, the place of sacrifice.[34] But it is also the place of revelation, of vocation. It is supremely the place of transfiguration, which is participation in the life of God.

It would be a serious misrepresentation to suggest that the meaning of the desert is to be found in the story of isolated individuals who are merely seeking their personal sanctification. There is, indeed, a strong emphasis upon the importance of the personal journey; but the High Priestly prayer serves as a necessary reminder that personal consecration is always – at least in part – for the sake of others.[35]

The transfiguration of which the desert speaks is never merely the accomplishment, the possession, even the grace of an individual. The counsel of Seraphim of Sarov,[36] a Russian Orthodox religious and hermit, was – 'Be at peace, and thousands around you will be saved'.[37] Few words are better able to convey the wider dimension, the wider consequences, of the process of transfiguration in which the individual is able to share – unseeing, unknowing – by virtue of his personal sanctification. To participate in the life of God is to participate in His continuing work of transfiguration.

There is, however, a prophetic tradition in the writings of the Old Testament which looks beyond our humanity and speaks of the day when the desert shall become like the garden of the Lord, a place of thanksgiving and the voice of song.[38] The breaking in of God's kingdom of righteousness must encompass a transformation of the whole created order. What is afforded by the desert experience now is some glimpse of the glory of God. Is this, then, the meaning of the word that the whole creation waits with eager longing for the revealing of the sons and daughters of God, because *only then* can the creation be set free from its bondage to decay and share in the glorious liberty of the children of God? [39]

The transfiguration of lives that are lived for God becomes, then, a sign, a promise, of the glory that shall be revealed. Beyond the story and the spirituality of the desert – solitude, testing, self-emptying, encounter, transfiguration – lies the mystery of God's redeeming purposes in which the whole creation will find its unity in Him.

AN ANTHOLOGY
FOR LENT

Ash Wednesday

THE CALL OF THE DESERT

Behold, I am doing a new thing ... for I give water in the wilderness, rivers in the desert, to give drink to my chosen people, the people whom I formed for myself that they might declare my praise.

Isaiah 43.18a, 20b–21

ASH WEDNESDAY

Setting Out On The Journey

1. What really matters is that I have taken the fundamental decision to begin the journey.

   Alessandro Pronzato

2. The desert is the threshold to the meeting ground of God and man. It is the scene of the exodus. You do not settle there, you pass through. One then ventures on to these tracks because one is driven by the Spirit towards the Promised Land. But it is only promised to those who are able to chew sand for forty years without doubting their invitation to the feast in the end.

   Alessandro Pronzato

3. The desert is a place where the soul encounters God, but it is also a place of extreme desolation – a place of testing, where the soul is flung upon its own resources and therefore upon God. The desert, in this sense, can be any where.

   Elizabeth Hamilton

4. The desert is both fascinating and terrifying. It is the great, lonely void, and human beings instinctively dread being brought face to face with themselves.

A Monk

5. The way you must go is the way you already know.

He has set it in your heart. The solitude will speak to you.

Derek Webster

6. Your call to the desert is as eternal as everything else concerning you, and it has its source in God's inexorable predilection for you.

A Monk

7. Open the first gate of the desert path that I may begin my journey.

Derek Webster

THURSDAY

The Inner Desert

1. For over three months I have laboured across the
   Sahara, and there have been few moments when I had
   experienced the magnetism of the desert to which so
   many people before me had succumbed. But now, in
   its utmost desolation, I began at last to understand its
   attraction. It was the awful scale of the thing, the
   suggestion of virginity, the fusion of pure elements from
   the heavens above and the earth beneath which were
   untrammelled and untouched by anything contrived by
   any human being.

   Geoffrey Moorhouse

2. There is a physical desert, inhabited by a few exceptional
   men and women who are called to live there; but more
   importantly, there is an inner desert, into which each one
   of us must one day venture. It is a void; an empty space
   for solitude and testing.

   Frère Ivan

3. For you, the desert is not a setting, it is a
   state of soul.

A Monk

4. Not everyone can or should live as a hermit. But no
   Christian can do without an inner hermitage in which to
   meet his God.

A Monk

5. The desert turns you inward.

A Monk

FRIDAY

The Presence And The Absence of God

1. The desert is an arid, scorching, frightening place where everything portends death. But at the same time it is also a place of rest, gentleness and life.

   In the desert you find friendliness and hostility, anguish and joy, sorrow and exultation, trial and triumph. The desert is the land of malediction and the land of benediction. The desert can be hard and merciless. You might die of thirst there, but if it rains you could be drowned. In the desert nature manifests itself in its extremes: prodigal fertility and cruel barrenness. We wait for years and do not get even a drop of rain. Then, without warning, the rain comes down in torrents; and, with frightening speed, the wadis fill up and overflow, sweeping everything before them. You might come upon an oasis where there is life and vegetation. And a little farther on you could find yourself on a desolate patch where you fear for your sanity.

   The desert can be tomb and cradle, wasteland and garden, death and resurrection, hell and heaven.

Thus in the desert you will find that God is simultaneously present and absent, proximate and remote, visible and invisible, manifest and hidden. He can receive you with great tenderness and then abandon you on the cross of loneliness. He consoles you and torments you at the same time. He heals you only to wound you again. He may speak to you today and ignore you tomorrow.

The desert does not delude and least of all does the desert delude those who accept it in its two-sided reality of life and death, presence and absence. Nor will they be deceived by God who calls them to the desert. God never abandons us.

Alessandro Pronzato

2. The desert is a good teacher. It is a place where we do not die of thirst. It is a place where we rediscover the roots of our existence. Once we grasp this lesson, we realise that the physical desert is not necessary to lead the life of a hermit. It then becomes pointless to go in search of a desert on the globe. You can find your desert in a corner of your house, on a motorway, in a square, in a crowded street. But you must first renounce the slavery of illusions, refuse the blackmail of pressure, resist the glitter of appearances, repudiate the domination of activity, reject the dictatorship of hypocrisy. Then the desert becomes a place where you do not go out to see the sand blowing in the wind but the Spirit waiting to make his dwelling within you.

Alessandro Pronzato

SATURDAY

Waiting Upon God

1. I have come into the desert to pray, to learn to pray.

   Prayer is the sum of our relationship with God.

   We are what we pray.
   Carlo Carretto

2. In the desert, God has marked out no other routes, no other paths than those of prayer.
   A Monk

3. In the desert the most urgent thing is – to wait.

   The desert does not take kindly to those who tackle it at breakneck speed, subjecting it to their plans and deadlines. It soon takes its revenge and makes them pay dearly for their presumption. Instead, the desert welcomes those who shed their sandals of speed and walk slowly in their barefeet, letting them be caressed and burnt by the sand.

   If you have no ambition to conquer the desert, if you do not think you are in charge, if you can calmly wait for things to be done, then the desert will not consider you an intruder and will reveal its secrets to you.
   Alessandro Pronzato

4. A desert spirituality is a spirituality of waiting upon God.
   There is an element of timelessness, of eternity, about the
   desert. The characteristic prayer of the desert is a prayer
   of simple waiting.

   David Prail

5. I have to walk the path to a deeper quiet in a hidden place.

   Derek Webster

First Sunday in Lent

SOLITUDE

When you pray, go into your room and shut the door and pray to your Father who is in secret, and your Father who sees in secret will reward you.

St Matthew 5.6

SUNDAY

Alone With God

1. The purpose of the spiritual quest of solitude is the Finding of God.

    Peter Anson

2. Let the desire to be with God goad you as often and as intensely as it may.

    A Monk

3. As soon as you are really alone you are with God.

    Thomas Merton

4. Seek to live alone with God and to live for God alone.

    Jean Leclerq

5. Except a man or woman shall say in their heart, I alone
   and God are in this world, they shall not find peace.

                                             Abbot Allois

6. He with whom God is
        is never less alone
      than when he is alone.

   For then he can enter his joy,
        then he is his own
   to enjoy God in himself
        and himself in God.

                                   William Saint-Thierry

MONDAY

The Solitude Of The Soul

1. Solitary places have always greatly helped the solitude of the soul.

   Jean Leclerq

2. I should be able to return to solitude each time as to the place I have never described to anybody, as the place which I have never brought anyone to see, as the place whose silence has mothered an interior life known to no one but God alone.

   Thomas Merton

3. Yet do not forget that you can be alone amid the noise of the world; and equally you can be surrounded by the hubbub of the world whilst withdrawn in your cell.

Theophan the Recluse

4. The desert ... taught me the distinction between solitude and isolation.

Alessandro Pronzato

5. Do not flee to solitude from the community. Find God first in the community, then He will lead you to solitude.

Thomas Merton

TUESDAY

Standing Before God

1. You seek the Lord? Seek, but only within yourself. He is not far from anyone. The Lord is near all those who truly call on Him. Find a place in your heart, and speak there with the Lord. It is the Lord's reception room. Everyone who meets the Lord meets Him there; he has fixed no other place for meeting souls.

   Theophan the Recluse

2. When you retreat into yourself, you should stand before the Lord, and remain in His presence, not letting the eyes of the mind turn away from the Lord. This is the true wilderness – to stand face to face with the Lord.

   Theophan the Recluse

3. As soon as a man or a woman is fully disposed to be alone with God, they are alone with God no matter where they may be.

At that moment they see that though they seem to be in the middle of their journey, they have already arrived at the end. For the life of grace on earth is the beginning of the life of glory. Although they are travellers in time, they have opened their eyes for a moment, in eternity.

Thomas Merton

WEDNESDAY

Waiting In Silence

1. Never be in a hurry. Do not expect to hear God's
   word immediately on your arrival in the desert.
   You must wait in silence. Your whole being should be
   in an attitude of listening. All other activities should
   be subordinated to the act of waiting for God. And
   God may speak through His word or through His
   silence.

   Alessandro Pronzato

2. Without silence, there is no solitude.

   Jean Leclerq

3. I find that silence teaches me more than
   many conversations.

   Jean Leclerq

4. It is in silence that we love most ardently; noise
   and words often put out the inner fire.

   Charles de Foucauld

5. Only silence of the heart allows us to reach the
   innermost secret of creation.

   Frère Ivan

6. The Father only utters one Word, that is to say, His Son,
   in an eternity of silence. He is saying it for ever. The
   soul too must hear it in silence.

   St John of the Cross

THURSDAY

The Deepest Silence

1. I said to my soul, be still, and wait without hope
   For hope would be hope for the wrong thing;
     wait without love.
   For love would be love of the wrong thing; there is
     yet faith.
   But the faith and the love and the hope are all in the
     waiting.
   Wait without thought, for you are not ready for thought;
   So the darkness shall be the light, and the stillness the
     dancing.

   T S Eliot

2. God's call is mysterious; it comes in the darkness of faith.
   It is so fine, so subtle, that it is only with the deepest
   silence within us that we can hear it.

   Carlo Carretto

3. In the crucible of silence you will learn holiness, since
   silence is the door to humility, contemplation and mercy.
   By leading you to self-forgetfulness, silence will allow you
   to discover God and in the heart of God you will
   rediscover the world by God's light.

   So live outward silence and enjoy it inwardly and you
   will taste the perfect delight of those who keep His
   commandments in their hearts and dwell silently in
   His love.

   Jerusalem Community : Rule of Life

4. You must put down your roots in silence. And this silence,
   more than any spoken word, will unite you to your
   fellow beings.

   Soeur Marie

FRIDAY

United With One Another

1. Holiness is life ... The solitude of a soul enclosed within itself is death. And so the authentic, the really sacred solitude is the infinite solitude of God, Himself, Alone.

   Thomas Merton

2. There is one Solitude in which all persons are at once together and alone.

   Thomas Merton

3. Men and women of solitude have discovered that the only way to be truly present to the world is to live in the presence of God.

   Alessandro Pronzato

4. The more we are alone with God the more we are united with one another.

   Thomas Merton

5. Solitude separates only to unite.

Brother Daniel-Ange

6. Solitude is genuine only when it is inhabited. And the best way not to have people in your way is to let them into your heart.

Alessandro Pronzato

7. The solitary cannot survive unless he is capable of loving everyone.

Thomas Merton

8. I have never loved nor prayed so much for my old friends as in the solitude of the desert. I saw their faces, I felt their problems, their sufferings, sharpened by the distance between us.

Carlo Carretto

SATURDAY

Finding The Truth

1. We fear to be alone, and be ourselves, and so to
   remind others of the truth that is in them.

   Thomas Merton

2. I have often said that the sole cause of our unhappiness
   is that we do not know how to stay quietly in our room.

   Blaise Pascal

3. The further I advance into solitude the more clearly I
   see the goodness of all things.

   Thomas Merton

4. Society depends for its existence on the inviolable
   personal solitude of its members.

   Thomas Merton

5. When society is made up of men and women who
   know no interior solitude it can no longer be held
   together by love.

   Thomas Merton

6. Mature religion as well as mature politics requires
   solitude.

   Thomas Merton

7. There will always be a place *for those isolated*
   consciences who have stood up for the universal
   conscience as against the mass mind. But their place
   is solitude. They have no other. Hence it is the solitary
   person (whether in the city or in the desert) who does
   humankind the inestimable favour of reminding it of its
   true capacity for maturity, liberty and peace.

   Thomas Merton

Second Sunday in Lent

TESTING

And Jesus, full of the Holy Spirit, returned from the Jordan, and was led by the Spirit for forty days in the wilderness, tempted by the devil.

St Luke 4.1–2a

SUNDAY

Constant Warfare

1. The desert offers a number of classic struggles, which you will be hard put to win; the desert's own excellent qualities provoke them.

   A Monk

2. Any one who is living in the desert is, in fact, at risk; the very extremity of their life-style quickly reduces them to extremes.

   Frère Ivan

3. The desert is the land of mirage, that seductive hallucination, the only defect of which is to be unreal.

   A Monk

4. Many acts of self-denial are heroic only in imagination, justified by some inaccessible ideal more dreamt than lived.

A Monk

5. The desert offers no respite. It prepares you for battle. The Promised Land is a place of war and peace at the same time. Anyone who prays does not only experience peace, they are also made to realise that the life of a Christian is a constant warfare. In this sense the experience of the desert takes you back to the point of departure, to your former environment, work and daily life. But the difference is that now you are a free person.

Alessandro Pronzato

6. When anyone penetrates deeper into the desert, they must take along with them faith, hope and charity. Their minds must be well made up and they must be firmly determined to achieve their goal. For combat will besiege them from every side.

A Desert Father

MONDAY

A Spirituality of Struggle

1. The life of the solitary will be a continual warfare, in which the flesh fights not only against the spirit but against the flesh itself and in which the spirit also fights not only against flesh but against the spirit.

   Thomas Merton

2. Demons belong to the desert, to the solitude of the desert.

   Andrew Louth

3. The desert is the country of madness ... it is the refuge of the devil ... thirst drives a person mad, and the devil himself is mad with a kind of thirst for his own lost excellence – lost because he has immured himself in it and closed out everything else.

   Thomas Merton

4. Not everyone is called to face the particular trials of
   St Antony but each one of us has, sooner or later, to
   confront the terrible demons which we carry inside: the
   demons of aggression, resentment, pride, sadness, despair.
                                                    Frère Ivan

5. Desert spirituality is a spirituality of struggle, which is
   inevitable as we seek to know and to journey into
   ourselves, to face the demons in the depths of our
   personalities. It is a struggle with the apparent absence
   of God and a struggle in the darkness of our own
   emptiness and insufficiency.
                                                    David Prail

6. The desert does not allow any compromise.
                                                    A Monk

TUESDAY

Total Confrontation

1. If some temptation arises in the place where you dwell
   in the desert, do not leave that place in time of
   temptation. For if you leave it then, no matter where you
   go, you will find the same temptation waiting for you.

   A Desert Father

2. Each person is tempted when they are lured and
   enticed by their own desires.

   Abbot Sisoes

3. If the inner man is not vigilant it is not possible to
   guard the outer man.

   A Desert Father

4. If you therefore go to the desert to be rid of all the
   dreadful people and all the awful problems in your life,
   you will be wasting your time. You should go to the
   desert for a total confrontation with yourself. For one
   goes to the desert to see more and to see better. One goes
   to the desert especially to take a closer look at the things
   and people one would rather not see, to face situations
   one would rather avoid, to answer questions one would
   rather forget.

   Alessandro Pronzato

5. The desert cell is Hell's cockpit, no less than a royal
   palace or the trader's bazaar, a maiden's thighs or the
   scholar's desk.

   But what is played out there takes its costume from the
   hidden thought of each actor. Shape and symbol are
   invested with power from conjoined dread and desire,
   both drawn from a soul's deepest wells.

   Derek Webster

WEDNESDAY

Learning Humility

1. If a person wants to, from morning 'til night,
   they can become like Christ; if they want to, they
   can also, from morning 'til night, become like
   the devil.

   A Desert Father

2. Your life is shaped by the end you live for.
   You are made in the image of what you desire.

   Thomas Merton

3. Just as bees are driven out by smoke, and their honey
   is taken away from them, so a life of ease drives out the
   fear of the Lord from a person's soul and takes away all
   their good works.

   Abbot Pastor

4. The Lord sometimes leaves in us some defects of character in order that we should learn humility. For without them we would immediately soar above the clouds in our own estimation and would place our throne there. And herein lies perdition.

Theophan the Recluse

5. It was said that one of the Desert Fathers had prayed to the Lord and the Lord had taken away all his passions, so that he became impassible. And in this condition he went to one of the elders and said, 'You see before you a man who is completely at rest and has no more temptations'. The elder said, 'Go and pray the Lord to command some struggle to be stirred up in you, for the soul is matured only in battles'. And when the temptations started up again he did not pray that the struggle be taken away from him, but only said, 'Lord, give me strength to get through the fight'.

Abbot Pastor

THURSDAY

Perseverance

1. Remain still. Do not desert your patch of sand.
   Bear the heat without and the cold within. Put
   up with the boredom of having nothing to do and
   the emptiness of having achieved nothing. Do not
   ask what you are accomplishing. What you
   accomplish is unimportant. Realise that the most
   extraordinary thing you can do is to pass the time
   which never passes. Hope can make time pass.
   Hope is indeed the true dimension of time. Time is
   also a factor in our exodus from the slavery of
   hurry to the promised land of hope.

Alessandro Pronzato

2. A hermit had persevered for thirty years. One day he said to himself, 'I have now spent so many years here and I have had no vision and performed no miracle as did the Fathers who were monks before me'. And he was tempted to go back into the world. Then he was told, 'What miracle do you want to perform that would be more extraordinary than the patience and courage God has given you and which allowed you to persevere for so long?'

A Desert Father

FRIDAY

Creative Action

1. The disciple of a great old man was once attacked
   by lust. The old man, seeing it in his prayer, said to him,
   'Do you want me to ask God to relieve you of this
   battle?' The other said, 'Abba, I see that I am afflicted,
   but I see that this affliction is producing fruit in me;
   therefore ask God to give me endurance to bear it'. And
   his Abba said to him, 'Today I know you surpass me in
   perfection'.

   A Desert Father

2. It is not because evil thoughts come to us that
   we are condemned, but only because we make
   use of the evil thoughts. It can happen that from
   these thoughts we suffer shipwreck, but it can also
   happen that because of them we may be crowned.

   A Desert Father

3. Christianity does not ask us to live in the shadow
   of the cross,
   but in the fire of its creative action.

   Teilhard de Chardin

SATURDAY

The Fruit of the Desert

1. From the moment Christ went out into the desert to
   be tempted, the loneliness, the temptation and the
   hunger of every man and woman became the loneliness,
   the temptation, and hunger of Christ.

   Thomas Merton

2. 'Love your enemies, do good to those who hate you,
   pray for those who treat you badly.' Grasping the
   meaning of these words needs maturity and also the
   experience of having come through inner deserts of
   our own.

   Brother Roger of Taizé

3. A soul untried by sorrows is good for nothing.

   Theophan the Recluse

4. If our emotions really die in the desert, our humanity dies
   with them. We must return from the desert like Jesus or
   St John, with our capacity for feeling expanded and
   deepened, strengthened against the appeals of falsity,
   warned against temptation, great, noble and pure.

   Thomas Merton

5. It was said of an old man that when his thoughts said
   to him, 'Relax today, and tomorrow repent', he replied,
   'No, I am going to repent today, and may the will of
   God be done tomorrow'.

   A Desert Father

Third Sunday in Lent

SELF-EMPTYING

And going a little further Jesus fell on His face
and prayed. 'My Father, if it be possible, let
this cup pass from me; nevertheless, not as I
will, but as thou wilt.'

St Matthew 16.39

SUNDAY

The Path Of Love

1. In the darkest night He is the One who can see the
   path along which to lead me.
   Carlo Carretto

2. The way lies on a path of love that has three gates:

   the failure of understanding,
   the forgetfulness of self and
   the remembrance of others.
   Derek Webster

3. The failure of understanding is the very track to God.
   Knowledge is not stones, but a voyage;
   Wisdom is not words, but a childlike heart;
   What stands at the forefront of the mind's stage,
   matters not a wrack.
   Recall rather summer's recesses and life's
   secret place.
   In a niche the mustard seed will grow.
   Anthony, Deacon in the Church of Ephesus

4. My Lord God, I have no idea where I am going. I do not
   see the road ahead of me. I cannot know for certain where
   it will end. Nor do I really know myself, and the fact that I
   think I am following Your will does not mean that I am
   actually doing so.

   But I believe that the desire to please You does in fact
   please You. And I hope I have that desire for all that I am
   doing. I hope that I will never do anything apart from that
   desire. And I know that if I do this You will lead me by the
   right road, though I may know nothing about it.

   Therefore I will trust You always though I may seem to be
   lost and in the shadow of death. I will not fear, for You are
   ever with me, and You will never leave me to face my
   perils alone.

   Thomas Merton

MONDAY

The Humility Of The Desert

1. Humility is the land where God wants us to go and offer sacrifice.

    Abbot Alonius

2. What have you to fear above all else?

    Self-satisfaction, self-appreciation, self-conceit, and all other things beginning with *self*.

    Work out your salvation with fear and trembling, kindle and maintain a contrite spirit, a humble and a contrite heart.

    Theophan the Recluse

3. Certain old men said, 'If thou seest a young man ascending by his own will up to heaven catch him by the foot and throw him down upon earth, for it is not expedient for him'.

    The Desert Fathers

4. A brother asked Abbot Sisois, saying, 'I know this of myself, that my mind is intent upon God'. And the old man said to him, 'It is no great matter that thy mind should be with God: but if thou didst see thyself less than any of His creatures, that were something'.

Abbot Sisois

5. Just as one cannot build a ship unless one has some nails, so it is impossible to be saved without humility.

Abbess Syncletica

TUESDAY

God Alone Is All

1. In order to arrive at having pleasure in everything, desire to have pleasure in nothing.

   St John of the Cross

2. The Abbot Joseph asked the Abbot Pastor, 'How should one fast?' Abbot Pastor said, 'I would have it so that every day one should deny oneself a little in eating, so as not to be satisfied'.

   Abbot Pastor

3. My true identity lies hidden in God's call to my freedom and my response to him.

   Thomas Merton

4. Be thou by nought perturbed
      Of nought afraid,
   For all things pass
      Save God,
   Who does not change.
   Be patient, and at last
      Thou shalt of all
   Fulfilment find.
      Hold God,
   And nought shall fail thee,
   For He alone is All.

St Teresa of Avila

WEDNESDAY

The Will To Love

1. Spend your life in the love of your neighbour.

   Charles de Foucauld

2. Love consists not in feeling that you love, but in the will to love.

   Charles de Foucauld

3. The Abbot Moses said, 'Unless people are convinced in their own hearts that they are sinners, God does not listen to their prayers'. Then one of the brethren said to him, 'What does it mean, this conviction in peoples' hearts that they are sinners?' The old man said to him, 'They who are conscious of their own sins have no eyes for the sins of their neighbour'.

   Abbot Moses

4. The desert teaches us that the love of neighbour is best
   practiced through renunciation rather than through
   self-realisation.

   Alessandro Pronzato

5. No one can enter into their deepest centre and pass
   through that centre into God, unless they are able to pass
   entirely out of themselves and empty themselves and give
   themselves to other people in the purity of a selfless love.

   Thomas Merton

THURSDAY

Resolute In Prayer

1. From the first we should be resolute in prayer.

St Teresa of Avila

2. When prayer dies, we die with it.

Frère Ivan

3. What is the use of praying if at the very moment of prayer we have so little confidence in God that we are busy planning our own kind of answer to our prayer?

Thomas Merton

4. The trouble, of course, is that we are so loath to admit our emptiness. We always want to have *something that is ours* to give. But perfection, even where prayer is concerned, lies in being able to accept one's indigence.

René Voillaume

5. Act as though everything depended upon you. But pray as though everything depended upon God.

St Ignatius

6. It is true that the solitary life must also be a life of prayer and meditation, if it is to be authentically Christian ... But what prayer! What meditation! ... Utter poverty. Often an incapacity to pray, to see, to hope ... a bitter, arid struggle to press forward through a blinding sandstorm.

Do not mistake my meaning. It is not a question of intellectual doubt ... It is something else, a kind of doubt that questions the very roots of a person's own existence, a doubt which undermines their very reasons for existing and for doing what they do. It is this doubt which reduces a person finally to silence, and in the silence which ceases to ask questions, they receive the only certitude they know: The presence of God in the midst of uncertainty and nothingness, as the only reality but as a reality which cannot be placed or identified.
                                        Thomas Merton

7. Lord, Jesus Christ, Son of God, have mercy upon me.
                                        The Jesus Prayer
                                        of the Orthodox Church

FRIDAY

The Darkness Of Faith

1. The more perfect faith is, the darker it becomes. The
closer we get to God, the less is our faith diluted with the
half-light of created images and concepts.

Thomas Merton

2. Why no! I never thought other than
That God is that great absence
In our lives, the empty silence
Within, the place where we go
Seeking, not in hope to
Arrive or find. He keeps the interstices
In our knowledge, the darkness
Between stars. His are the echoes
We follow, the footprints he has just
Left. We put our hands in
His side hoping to find
It warm. We look at people
And places as though he had looked
At them, too; but miss the reflection.

R.S. Thomas

3. We have to come face to face with the absence of God.
There are various refuges ... they may be inhabited, we
may stay with them, but we have to know that they are
not where we have to go. In the end, if we are fortunate,
we will come to a point where there is a wilderness, an
emptiness, and no way forward. Here we have to trust
and allow ourselves to be found in God and to be content
with that.

Thomas Merton

4. The experience of prayer in the desert shows that what we
   normally consider light is our own light, not God's. The
   desert requires us to put out our pale little flame. Then, in
   the absence of human lights, our eyes will get used to the
   brightness of God's light. Darkness there is the
   prerequisite for seeing. It then becomes futile to attempt to
   see God's light with the aid of our light. All too readily we
   cry out, 'Lord, grant that I may see!' But few of us seem
   prepared to receive the gift of sight through the painful
   process of becoming blind first.

   Alessandro Pronzato

5. God, who is everywhere, never leaves us. Yet, He
   seems sometimes to be present, sometimes absent.
   If we do not know him well, we do not realise that
   He may be more present to us when He is absent
   than when He is present.

   Thomas Merton

SATURDAY

Giving God Everything

1. The desert loves those who renounce themselves.
   Alessandro Pronzato

2. Before we can surrender ourselves we must become
   ourselves. No one can give up what they do not possess.
   Thomas Merton

3. How many ways do you think there are of loving? How
   many ways are there of giving oneself? There is only one:
   the strong way, the complete way, the heroic way. Of
   those who really mean to serve Him, Jesus requires
   nothing less.
   René Voillaume

4. ... when all love, all longing, all desire, all seeking, all
   thoughts of ours, all that we see, all that we say, all that
   we hope, shall be God.
   John Cassian

5. I want to give God everything.
   Thomas Merton

6. My Father
   I abandon myself to you,
   Do with me as you will.
   Whatever you may do with me
   I thank you.
   I am prepared for anything,
   I accept everything
   Provided your will is fulfilled in me
   And in all creatures.
   I ask for nothing more
   my God.
   I place my soul in your hands.
   I give it you, my God,
   with all the love of my heart
   because I love you.
   And for me it is a necessity of love,
   this gift of myself,
   this placing of myself in your hands
   without reserve
   in boundless confidence,
   because you are
   my Father.

Charles de Foucauld

Fourth Sunday in Lent

ENCOUNTER

'Now is my soul troubled. And what shall I say? "Father, save me from his hour?" No, for this purpose I have come to this hour. Father, glorify thy name.'

St John 12.27

SUNDAY

The Discoveries Of The Desert

1. Yesterday, you understood a little; today, you understand
   better; tomorrow, you will understand better still: the
   light of God is growing in you.

   St Augustine of Hippo

2. How may He who is eternally present,
       absent Himself?
   How may He who is heard in each sound,
       silence Himself?
   How may He who is in all motion,
       still Himself?
   How may the One whose being is love,
       cease from loving?

   Derek Webster

3. In the desert you discover your true name, and
   God calls you by that name.

   Alessandro Pronzato

4. Have I succeeded in making my desert in the city? I do not know. But now I do not think of the desert in geographical terms. The desert is all around me and within me. I think of it now as an essential dimension of life, the natural habitat for Christians.

Perhaps God is not partial to the city or the desert. What might interest Him on His strolls in our cities could be to find oases of spirituality where there are individuals capable of waiting and hoping instead of hurrying and worrying.

Alessandro Pronzato

5. An old man said, 'If someone lives in a place and does not reap the fruit which that place affords it will drive him away because he has not known how to work there'.

A Desert Father

6. Divine joy is a delicate thing which is not given to one who seeks any other.

St Bernard of Clairvaux

MONDAY

Desiring God

1. I fear for the man who no longer knows where
   his God is.

   Carlo Caretto

2. What then do you wish to know?

   I desire to know God and the soul.

   Nothing more?

   Nothing whatever.

   St Augustine of Hippo

3. Whether you understand it or not, God loves you, is
   present to you, lives in you, dwells in you, calls you,
   saves you.

   Thomas Merton

4. No desire has arisen in my heart for anything
   except God.

   Abbot Souros

5. God does not give His joy to us for ourselves alone,
   and if we could possess Himself for ourselves alone, we
   would not possess Him at all. Any joy that does not
   overflow from our souls and help other people to rejoice
   in God does not come to us from God.

   Thomas Merton

TUESDAY

Discerning Jesus

1. The Gospel is everything.

   The Gospel is a living person: Jesus Christ.
   Carlo Carretto

2. Whoever findeth Jesus findeth a good treasure, yea, a
   Good above all good.
   St Thomas à Kempis

3. Christ be with me, Christ within me,
   Christ behind me, Christ before me,
   Christ beside me, Christ to win me,
   Christ to comfort and restore me,
   Christ beneath me, Christ above me,
   Christ in quiet, Christ in danger,
   Christ in hearts of all that love me,
   Christ in mouth of friend and stranger.
   St Patrick

4. I want to preach the Gospel with my life.

Charles de Foucauld

5. For the spreading of the Gospel, I am ready to go to the ends of the Earth and I am likewise ready to live till the day of judgement.

Charles de Foucauld

WEDNESDAY

Finding Ourselves

1. The things that we love tell us what we are.

   Thomas Merton

2. Not to accept and love and do God's will is to
   refuse the fullness of my existence.

   Thomas Merton

3. Try to enter the treasure chamber ... that is within you
   and then you will discover the treasure chamber of
   heaven. For they are one and the same. If you succeed in
   entering one you will see both. The ladder to this
   Kingdom is hidden inside you, in your soul.

   Isaac the Syrian

4. There is only one problem on which all my existence, my
   peace and my happiness depend: to discover myself in
   discovering God. If I find Him, I will find myself; and if I
   find my true self, I will find Him.

   Thomas Merton

5. A door opens in the centre of our being and we seem to
   fall through it into immense depths which, although they
   are infinite, are all accessible to us; all eternity seems to
   have become ours in this one placid and breathless
   contact. God touches us with a touch that is emptiness
   and empties us. He moves us with a simplicity that
   simplifies us. All variety, all complexity, all paradox, all
   multiplicity cease. Our mind swims in the air of an
   understanding, a reality that is dark and serene and
   includes in itself everything. Nothing more is desired ...
   you feel as if you were at last fully born. All that went
   before was a mistake, a fumbling preparation for birth ...
   And yet now you have become nothing, you have sunk to
   the centre of your own poverty, and there you have felt the
   doors fly open into infinite freedom, into a wealth that is
   perfect because none of it is yours, and yet it all belongs to
   you.

   Thomas Merton

THURSDAY

Loving Our Neighbour

1. I must look for my identity somehow, not only
   in God but in other people.

   Thomas Merton

2. Do not be afraid that an increase in your personal love
   for God will in any way diminish your love for your
   neighbour. On the contrary, it will enrich it.

   Carlo Carretto

3. The foundation is our neighbour.

   John the Dwarf

4. Our life and our death are with our neighbour.

St Antony

5. We laughed together in the desert, we who shared neither language nor country, race nor creed; only our humanity did we share and that was enough.

Edward Edwards

6. Be a friend to all, a brother to all. Be little, be universal.

Charles de Foucauld

FRIDAY

Emerging From The Shadows

1. We and our world interpenetrate. If anything, the world
   exists for us, and we exist for ourselves. It is only in
   assuming full responsibility for our world, for our lives
   and for ourselves, that we can be said to live really for
   God.

   Thomas Merton

2. In the heart of anguish are found the gifts of peace and
   understanding: not simply in personal illumination and
   liberation, but by commitment and empathy, for the
   contemplative must assume the universal anguish and the
   inescapable condition of mortal man.

   Thomas Merton

3. Contemplatives thrust straight into the world and the
   world's misery.

   Jacques and Raisse Maritain

4. The crowded bus, the long queue, the railway platform, the traffic jam, the neighbours' television sets, the heavy-footed people on the floor above you, the person who still keeps getting the wrong number on your phone. These are the real conditions of your desert. Do not allow yourself to be irritated. Do not try to escape. Do not postpone your prayer. Kneel down. Enter that disturbed solitude. Let your silence be spoilt by those sounds. It is the beginning of your desert.

Alessandro Pronzato

5. The poorest of the poor; the most repellent; a child newly born; a failing old man; the least intelligent of human beings; the most abandoned; an imbecile; a dullard; a sinner; the greatest of sinners; the most ignorant; the lowest of the low; the person who is the most repugnant, physically or morally – each is a child of God, a Son of the Most High.

Charles de Foucauld

6. If you are generous, little by little you will see the divine world emerging from the shadows. You have been living in it unawares, the hurly-burly of the world not having allowed it to be seen. You then in your turn will wonderingly discover that you are never less alone than when you are alone.

A Monk

SATURDAY

The Healing Power of God

1. To desire God is to pray.

   René Voillaume

2. Prayer ... is not a rejection of the present; it is rather a realisation that the present is not enough.

   Alessandro Pronzato

3. Those who pray
   stand at that point
   of intersection
   where the love of God
   and the tensions and
   sufferings we inflict
   on each other
   meet and are held
   in the healing power of God.

   Mother Mary Clare

4. Prayer is the test of everything; prayer is also the source
   of everything; prayer is the driving force of everything;
   prayer is also the direction of everything. If prayer is right,
   everything is right. For prayer will not allow anything to
   go wrong.

   Theophan the Recluse

TRANSFIGURATION

The wilderness and the dry land shall be glad, the desert shall rejoice and blossom; like the crocus it shall blossom abundantly, and rejoice with joy and singing ... They shall see the glory of the Lord, the majesty of our God ... For waters shall break forth in the wilderness, and streams in the desert; the burning sand shall become a pool, and the thirsty ground springs of water ... And a highway shall be there, and it shall be called the Holy Way ... And the ransomed of the Lord shall return, and come to Zion with singing.

Isaiah 35.1–2, 6–8, 10

SUNDAY

Entering The Promised Land

1. The exodus from slavery to freedom takes place in
   the desert.
   > *Carlo Carretto*

2. It is not enough to leave Egypt, one must also enter the
   Promised Land.
   > *St John Chrysostom*

3. A fresh kind of life is starting.
   > *Teilhard de Chardin*

4. John's thoughts moved to the time that he and Nicholas
   had first met. Travelling through the wastes of Scete, the
   Abbot had asked for shelter in his cell. That night John
   was born anew. Nicholas had

   > loosed a mind too tied by prayer,
   > freed a spirit from destructive dogma,
   > fed a body too full of fasting
   >   and let him laugh.
   >> *Abbot Nicholas and John the Dwarf*
   >> *Derek Webster*

5. It is worth any sacrifice,
   however great or costly,
   to see eyes that were listless,
   light up again;
   to see someone smile
   who seemed to have forgotten
   how to smile;
   to see trust reborn
   in someone
   who no longer believed
   in anything
   or Anyone.

Dom Helder Camara

MONDAY

Being Transformed by Love

1. HE IS — and this reality absorbs everything else.
                                                    Thomas Merton

2. The desert in its dryness, the night in its annihilation
   of forms, speaks less of God's generosity than of His
   transcendent affection. It is not sufficient for you to know
   about this in theory. You have to experience it and freely
   yield this homage to love.
                                                    A Monk

3. God is love and if the soul dwells in love, God is in it
   and it is in His love, so that God becomes the all in all.
                                                    Jean Leclerq

4. God does not hurry over things; time is His, not mine, and I, little creature, have been called to be transformed into God by sharing His life. And what transforms me is the charity which he pours into my heart. Love transforms me slowly into God.

Carlo Carretto

5. The limit of our love for God should be to love Him without limit.

St Bernard of Clairvaux

6. The soul lives by love: but it does not live in itself, nor does it live in God, nor does God live in it. God alone lives in God, and the soul lives by the very fact that it is transformed in God, when it lives neither itself in itself, nor itself in God, nor God in itself, but only God in God. These words 'God in God' are a constantly recurring refrain, the clue to the whole mystery of hermit life: God alone in God. *Solo Dio in Dio.*

Jean Leclerq

TUESDAY

The Desert Flower

1. Whenever doubts and the silences of God
   seem to deepen, will you look to discern the
   desert flower?

   Brother Roger of Taizé

2. Sometimes the landscape of my soul
   seems like this burnt hillside,
   the wind rattling orange leaves on black twigs,
   the soil full of ash between the stones.
   Sometimes the landscape of my soul
   seems like this terrible waste of dead trees.

   Walking this afternoon among the charred remains
   I found a black stump sprouting leaves
   and new grass thinly veiling
   a delicate oak sapling
   in this, the ravaged landscape of my soul.

   Susan Fisher

3. I ask for riches.
    You gave me the earth, the sea,
            the immensity
    of the broad sky. I looked at them
    and learned I must withdraw
        to possess them. I gave my eyes
        and my ears, and dwelt
    in a soundless darkness
            in the shadow
            of your regard.
            The soul
        grew in me, filling me
    with its fragrance.
            Men came
    to me from the four
        winds to hear me speak
        of the unseen flower by which
    I sat, whose roots were not
    in the soil, nor its petals the colour
    of the wide sea; that was
        its own species with its own
        sky over it, shot
    with the rainbow of your coming and going.

    R.S. Thomas

WEDNESDAY

Encountering God

1. It is small advantage for eyes to see
      if the heart is blind.
   The great world brims over with His glory,
      yet He may only dwell
   where a person chooses to give Him entrance.

   Abbot Nicholas

2. I seem now to have reached a means of encountering Him
   in a way I have never known before.

   And this meeting between God's totality and man's
   nothingness is the greatest wonder of creation ... It is the
   truth of God and man.

   Carlo Carretto

3. If a man or woman is to live, they must be all alive,
   body, soul, mind, heart, spirit. Everything must be
   elevated and transformed by the action of God, in love
   and faith.

   Thomas Merton

4. If God does not glorify a human being, the glory of people is without value.

Abbot Sisoes

5. Abba Lot came to Abba Joseph and said: 'Father, according as I am able, I keep my little rule, and my little fast, my prayer and meditation and contemplative silence; and according as I am able I strive to cleanse my heart of thoughts. Now what more should I do?'

The elder rose up in reply and stretched out his hands to heaven, and his fingers became like ten lamps of fire. He said: 'Why not be totally changed into fire?'

Abbot Joseph

6. The glory of God is a man or a woman who is truly alive.

St Irenaeus

THURSDAY

Sanctifying The World

1. If you see a person pure and humble, that is a great
   vision. For what is greater than such a vision, to see
   the invisible God in a visible man or woman.

   St Pachomius

2. Every moment and every event of every person's
   life on earth plants something in their soul ... If I
   were looking for God, every event and every moment
   would sow, in my will, grains of His life, that would
   spring up one day in a tremendous harvest.

   Thomas Merton

3. The human heart is the focal point from which history
   must be transfigured; only the sanctified human being can
   sanctify the world.

   Frère Ivan

4. My chief care should not be to find pleasure or success, health or life or money or rest or even things like virtue and wisdom – still less their opposites, pain, failure, sickness, death. But in all that happens my one desire and my one joy should be to know: 'Here is the thing that God has willed for me. In this His love is found, and in accepting this I can give back His love to Him and give myself with it to Him'.

And by receiving His will with joy and doing it with gladness I have His love in my heart because my will is now the same as His love and I am on the way to becoming what He is, who is Love. And by accepting all things from Him, I receive His joy into my soul, not because things are what they are but because God is who He is and His love has willed my joy in them all.

Thomas Merton

FRIDAY

Having Nothing

1. Reflect, my son, Do you walk too quickly for God?

    Hear that song which the Lord sings with your life.
    Recall that:
      There is one time for the lattices of heaven
      to give dew,
      And another for the sun to fire the sands.
      There is one time for children to play with
      coloured toys,
      And another when they rest upon their
      pallets.
      There is a time when life blooms and
      youth is all,
      And another when white hairs close
      life's door.

    Reflect again my son, Do you climb too high for God?

    Recall that a solitary:
      Seeks not the voice of God, but hears
      it in cracking ice, blowing reeds
      and brethren's laughter.
      Seeks not the gifts of God, but
      finds them in new bread, the
      darkness of dawn and brethren's love.
      Seeks not the vision of God, but
      spies His Print on bee's wing,
      fishes' fin and brother's heart.

Reflect again my son. Do you ask too much of God?

Know that:
    When His prize is downfalling, you
    may find a rising.
    When His favour is silence, you may
    catch a melody.
    When His blessing is suffering, you
    may sense deep peace.

So:
    The heart of darkness is new light.
    The heart of despair is fresh hope.
    The heart of death is eternal life.

Only those who have nothing can
    accept everything.

Abbot Nicholas and John the Dwarf
Derek Webster

SATURDAY

Participation In God

1. Christians are not trying to steal something from God that God does not want them to have.

   On the contrary, they are striving with their whole heart to fulfill the will of God and lay hands upon that which God created them to receive.

   And what is that?

   It is nothing else but a participation in the life, and wisdom, and joy and peace of God Himself.

   Thomas Merton

2. We are poor, possessing all things. Having nothing of our
   own left to rely on, we have nothing to lose and nothing to
   fear. Everything is locked away for sure possession,
   beyond our reach, in Heaven. We live where our souls
   desire to be, and our bodies no longer matter very much.
   We are buried in Christ, our life is hidden with Christ in
   God, and we know the meaning of His freedom.

   Thomas Merton

THE DIVINE MYSTERY

For God has made known to me in all wisdom and insight the mystery of His will, according to His purpose which He set forth in Christ as a plan for the fullness of time, to unite all things in Him, things in heaven and things on earth.

Ephesians 1.9–10

PALM SUNDAY

Going To Jerusalem

1. When the days drew near for Him to be received up, He
   set his face to go to Jerusalem.

   St Luke 9.51

2. Whoever says God in the sense of Holy Scripture will
   necessarily have to say Jesus Christ over and over again.

   Karl Barth

3. If the truth of God is disclosed and the glory of God is
   manifest in Jesus, then the truth of God must be this and
   the glory of God must appear in this – that God so
   initiates and acts that He destines Himself to enter into
   passion, to wait and to receive.

   W.H. Vanstone

4. And God held in his hand
   A small globe. Look, he said.
   The son looked. Far off,
   As through water, he saw
   A scorched land of fierce
   Colour. The light burned
   There; crusted buildings
   Cast their shadows: a bright
   Serpent, a river
   Uncoiled itself, radiant
   With slime.

   On a bare
   Hill a bare tree saddened
   The Sky. Many people
   Held out their thin arms
   To it, as though waiting
   For a vanished April
   To return to its crossed
   Boughs. The son watched
   Them. Let me go there, he said.

                                    R.S. Thomas

MONDAY IN HOLY WEEK

Loving The Cross

1. And when He drew near and saw the city He wept
    over it, saying, 'Would that even today you knew the
    things that make for peace! But now they are hid from
    your eyes'.

    St Luke 19.41–2

2. There is but one road to the kingdom of God – a cross,
    voluntary or involuntary.

    Theophan the Recluse

3. The desert teaches us how to carry our cross alone and in the steps of the Lord, as He carried His alone.

A Monk

4. Ask for the privilege of loving the Cross.

A Monk

TUESDAY IN HOLY WEEK

The Land of Sacrifice

1. Truly, truly, I say to you, unless a grain of wheat falls
   into the earth and dies, it remains alone; but if it dies,
   it bears much fruit.

   St John 12.24

2. The desert ... is the chosen land of sacrifice ... Instead
   of the garden of delights, the steppe; instead of leafy trees,
   the Cross. Man lost himself in the earthy paradise; he
   redeems himself in the wilderness. The Cross is the true
   tree of life.

   A Monk

3. I have received the cross. I have received it from Thy hand.
   I will bear it, and bear it even unto death, as Thou hast
   laid it upon me.

   St Thomas à Kempis

4. They who enter the way of life in faith bear the cross
   patiently. They who advance in hope bear the cross
   readily. They who are perfected in charity embrace the
   cross ardently.

   St Bernard of Clairvaux

WEDNESDAY IN HOLY WEEK

Wholeness And Finality

1. I came to cast fire on the earth; and would that it
   were already kindled! I have a baptism to be baptised
   with; and how I am constrained until it is accomplished!
   St Luke 12.49–50

2. There is something in the depths of our being that hungers
   for wholeness and finality. Because we are made for
   eternal life, we are made for an act that gathers up all the
   powers and capacities of our being and offers them
   simultaneously and for ever to God.
   Thomas Merton

3. The death of Jesus is a mystery wrought in the silence of God.

St Ignatius of Antioch

4. *Crux omnia probat.*

The cross tests everything.

Martin Luther

MAUNDY THURSDAY

The Hour Of The Garden

1. My Father, if it be possible, let this cup pass from me;
   nevertheless, not as I will, but as thou wilt.

   St Matthew 27.39b

2. In the fortunate night
   In secret, seen by none
   And seeing nothing
   Having no other light or guide
   Than that which burned in my heart.

   It guided me, this light,
   More surely than the light of noon
   To the place where he
   Whom I knew well
   Waited for me,
   A place where there was
   No one to be seen.

   St John of the Cross

3. Now is the hour of the garden and the night, the hour
   of the silent offering: *therefore the hour of hope*: God
   alone. Faceless, unknown, unfelt, yet undeniably God.

   Abbé Monchanin

4. At midnight I awoke and gazed up to heaven.
    No star of all the starry host
    Smiled down upon me at midnight.
    At midnight my thoughts went out into the bounds
    of darkness.
    No light brought me thoughts of comfort
    At midnight.
    At midnight I noted the beating of my heart;
    I felt a single pang of pain.
    At midnight.
    At midnight I fought the battle of human woe;
    but with all my power I could not decide it.
    At midnight.
    At midnight I gave the power into thy hand.
    Lord, thou keepest watch over life and death,
    At midnight.

Freidrich Ruckert

GOOD FRIDAY

The Sacrifice Of God

1. Now is my soul troubled. And what shall I say?
   'Father save me from this hour?' No, for this purpose
   I have come to this hour. Father, glorify thy name.
   St John 12.27–8a

2. God shows His love for us in that while we were
   yet sinners Christ died for us.
   Romans 5.8

3. My God, my God, why hast thou forsaken me?
   St Mark 15.34

4. It is accomplished.
   St John 19.30

5. Now is the judgement of this world, now shall the
   rulers of this world be cast our; and I, when I am
   lifted up from the earth, will draw all men to myself.
   St John 12.31–2

6. Morning glory, starlit sky,
   Leaves in springtime, swallows' flight,
   Autumn gales, tremendous seas,
   Sounds and scents of summer night;

   Soaring music, tow'ring words,
   Art's perfection, scholar's truth,
   Joy supreme of human love,
   Memory's treasure, grace of youth;

   Open, Lord, are these, Thy gifts,
   Gifts of love to mind and sense;
   Hidden is love's agony,
   Love's endeavour, love's expense.

   Love that gives gives ever more,
   Gives with zeal, with eager hands,
   Spares not, keeps not, all outpours,
   Ventures all, its all expends.

   Drained is love in making full;
   Bound in setting others free;
   Poor in making many rich;
   Weak in giving power to be.

   Therefore He Who Thee reveals
   Hangs, O Father, on that Tree
   Helpless; and the nails and thorns
   Tell of what Thy love must be.

   Thou art God; no monarch Thou
   Thron'd in easy state to reign;
   Thou art God, Whose arms of love
   Aching, spent, the world sustain.

   W.H. Vanstone

EASTER EVE

Descending Into Nothingness

1. You have died and your life is hid with Christ in God.
    Colossians 3.3

2. Simply waiting for God in silence *is* prayer.
    Ladislaus Boros

3. Hope then is a gift ... total, unexpected,
    incomprehensible, undeserved ... but to meet it, we have
    to descend into nothingness.

    It is the acceptance of life in the midst of death, not
    because we have courage, or light, or wisdom to accept,
    but because by some miracle the God of life Himself
    accepts to live, in us, at the very moment when we descend
    into death.
    Thomas Merton

4. Be awake, thou sleeping one. Rise from Death to
   Light.

He, who left the heavens, for the dust of earth,
He, who took the spittle down His face,
   received the blows upon His cheeks.
He, who slept upon a cross'd tree, embroidered in
   His red:
Came to Death to bring you life.

Be awake, thou sleeping one, Rise from Death to
   Light.

The cherubim have unbarred the gates of Paradise.
The throne is hewn and decked.
A banquet ready, everlasting chambers are
   prepared.
The treasure chest being split, a kingdom awaits
   thee.
Awake! Arise!

Derek Webster

EASTER DAY

The Song Of The Desert

1. I have been crucified with Christ; it is no longer I who
   live, but Christ who lives in me.

   Galatians 2.20

2. Among the sons of men the Lord Jesus only has
   appeared, in whom all have been crucified, all are
   dead and buried, all again have been raised.

   The Leo the Great

3. Can that ecstasy of love
       In which one life is welcomed by All Life;
       In which one song is encircled by All Singing;
       In which one soul is girded with Eternal Life;
          Be set down in letters?

   It is a poem which only His tongue can utter
   And the ears of those whom he has
       blessed received.

   Derek Webster

4. The end of man is endless Godhead endlessly possessed.

   Austin Farrer

5. *Alleluia* is the song of the desert.

Thomas Merton

THE LITERATURE
OF THE DESERT

Much has been done in the course of this century to make the wisdom of the Desert Fathers of the early centuries easily accessible, and not least of all through the writings of James Hannay,[1] Helen Waddell,[2] Thomas Merton,[3] and Benedicta Ward.[4] But behind the anthologies compiled by these writers there lies a rich tradition of literature which encapsulates the story and the spirituality of the desert.

The *Lives* of some of the early Desert Fathers – Antony,[5] Paul of Thebes,[6] Pachomius[7] – provide the first accounts of these pioneers of the desert tradition and of the monastic settlements in the Egyptian desert with which they were associated. Collections of stories and sayings had undoubtedly been brought together before the end of the fourth century, prior to the compilation of the larger collections by travellers in the fifth century.

It is certainly from the fourth quarter of the fifth century that *The Sayings of the Fathers*[8] have come down, drawing together random collections of stories and spiritual maxims. These had obviously been adapted in the course of recording and re-telling, but they constitute the bed-rock of the written tradition. Their importance lies in the spiritual value of the words which were originally addressed to specific individuals and particular situations, but they continue to speak with a refreshing simplicity and compulsion.

Early travellers to the desert included Basil the Great, Rufinus of Aquileia, Melania, Jerome, Palladius, and John Cassian. Some of these travellers contributed to *The Sayings*; but other writings – the *Lausiac History*[9] and the *Historia Monachorum in Aegypto*[10] – provide us with a picture of monastic life in the desert which, in spite of the piety and the nostalgia that are to be found in some places in the telling of the story, possess a character which is both informative and authentic.

The writings of St Athanasius became a primary, a seminal influence in the thinking of Western monasticism, and especially through his *Life of St Antony*. But his writings were complemented by John Cassian who through his

Conferences[11] and Institutes[12] transmitted the desert tradition to the mainstream of Benedictine monasticism in the
western church. The *Rule of Pachomius*[13] which had served
as a model for St Basil the Great, was translated into Latin by
Jerome at the beginning of the fifth century. It was Jerome's
achievement to ensure that the ascetical tradition spread into
Italy and around the Mediterranean and into Gaul. It was,
however, *St Benedict*[14] who gave shape and direction to western monasticism, but his *Rule*[15] – like the *Rule* of St Basil and
the *Institutes* of John Cassian – derived in large measure
from the accumulated and interpreted experiences of the
early desert communities.

Monasticism became the custodian of the desert tradition
in the churches of the west and of the east, although it is in
the life of the anchorites that the spirituality of the Desert
Fathers has been most conspicuously taken forward in the
eastern church. Vladimir Lossky provides in *The Mystical
Theology of the Eastern Church*[16] a primary work of reference for all who would explore the character of Orthodoxy
and its points of departure from the theological tradition of
the west. Lossky does not address specifically the experiences
of the Desert Fathers but he sets all expositions of Christian
faith and life within the broad frame of Orthodoxy, in which
theology and mysticism inform and complement each other;
in which grace and human freedom are held together; in
which everything is subordinate to the end of the Christian
life, which is union with God.

But nothing can better testify to the familiarity and the
consistency of the desert tradition – in both the east and the
west – than *The Art of Prayer : An Orthodox Anthology*.[17]
The subject matter of this unique book is prayer, and especially the *Jesus Prayer*. It was compiled by Fr Igumen
Chariton, a Russian Orthodox monk, in the mid-1930s, so
that he might bring within the reach of people those writings
within the Orthodox tradition which had assisted him on his
monastic journey. It draws substantially upon the writings of
two Russian Orthodox bishops, Theophan the Recluse and
Ignatii Brianchaninov, in the second half of the nineteenth

century, but it goes back to the fourth century in order to set out 'the spiritual teaching of the Orthodox Church in its classic and traditional form'.[18]

A comprehensive account of the story of the solitary life in the Christian church from the earliest times down to the present century is to be found in Peter Anson's book, *The Call of the Desert*.[19] It makes no attempt to provide a rationale of lives that are lived in silence and solitude, beyond the conviction that for those who are so called it is the one thing that is necessary.

It is the necessity of this vocation within the life of the church that is the burden of Thomas Merton's *Preface* to Jean Leclercq's important book, *Alone with God*.[20] Merton's conviction is quite simply that the Kingdom of God is incomplete without hermits because they alone seek God with 'the most absolute and undaunted and uncompromising singleness of heart'.[21]

His *Preface* serves, however, as a commendation to Leclercq's significant achievement in bringing before the reader the teaching of Paul Giustiniani, who established a community of hermits in Italy early in the sixteenth century. Giustiniani's writings, which have been largely unpublished, have at their heart his understanding of the spiritual life. His *Rules* for the ordering of his community[22] addressed every aspect of the eremitic life. Leclercq's book makes available Giustiniani's understanding of the vocation of the hermit, his role, his life, his prayer, his asceticism and his goal. The vocation is summed up in the words – 'Seek to live alone with God and to live for God alone'.[23]

Few twentieth century writers have shown a keener appreciation of these things than Thomas Merton. Certainly his exposition of solitude and of the solitary life in his *Notes for a Philosophy of Solitude*,[24] written in the light of his own monastic journey, stands alongside the classic texts of the desert tradition. There is a timeless quality about the literature of the spirituality of the desert which enables it to transcend the many different ways in which the ideal of the desert has found expression.

No brief examination of the literature of the desert can ignore the spiritual writings and poetry of St John of the Cross.[25] The claim that he should take his place among the exponents of the desert tradition does not rest upon the outer, visible circumstances of his life. It rests, rather, upon all that his writings tell us about his interior life. The *Ascent of Mount Carmel*, the *Dark Night*, the *Living Flame of Love*, the *Spiritual Canticle* – these are the writings which, employing the images that properly belong to the desert, speak of the encounter of God and the soul in love.

The writings of St John of the Cross speak eloquently of the mystical tradition of prayer in which he stood. The writings of some of our twentieth century poets – and T.S. Eliot[26] and R.S. Thomas[27] are the two who come most obviously to mind – draw upon the experience of the desert in order to convey something of the alienation of our world and of the apparent absence of God which is inseparable from discipleship.

T.S. Eliot, mindful of the burden of human suffering, speaks of the desert in *The Waste Land* as a source of meaning. The frustrations of personal relationships are depicted in *The Family Reunion* in terms of the 'solitude that can be found in a crowded desert'. Eliot is the most eclectic of writers, drawing freely upon a vast range of sources in order to secure the association of ideas, the resonances, that he requires. His *Four Quartets* include quotations from and references to St John of the Cross (*East Coker*) and Julian of Norwich (*Little Gidding*); while his reference in *Murder in the Cathedral* to 'the death in the desert, the prayer in forgotten places' has been taken by many to be an allusion to Charles de Foucauld.

R.S. Thomas does not use the language of the desert, but he expresses repeatedly in his poetry something of the truth of the desert tradition. God is experienced as 'that great absence in our lives'; He is 'the empty silence within, the place where we go seeking' (*Via Negativa*). But the absence and the silence have their own fascination, their own compulsion; and in the emptiness of our experience there is the silent offering of 'A vacuum He may not abhor' (*The Absence*). It is, of course, an inward journey that is required (*Groping*); and the invariable experience of the desert tradition of prayer is confirmed by the quiet recognition that 'the meaning is in the waiting' (*Kneeling*).

A helpful study of desert spirituality is provided by Andrew Louth in his book *The Wilderness of God*.[28] He does not attempt a systematic survey of the desert tradition in Christian spirituality, but he provides a series of studies which show how the tradition has manifested itself in different people, at different times, and in different settings.

It is one of the paradoxes of the contemporary world that a blatant secularity should be accompanied by a rediscovery of the desert tradition. Such a tradition will be unknown to large numbers of people, as surely as the lives of the early Desert Fathers were unknown to many of their contemporaries. But nothing is ultimately hidden; nothing is ultimately unrelated; nothing is ultimately lost.

This fundamental theological affirmation has been verified yet again through the life of Charles de Foucauld and the work of the many communities that derive their inspiration from him. The story of de Foucauld's hopes for his desert community is set out in his *Letters from the Desert*;[29] and a wide-ranging exposition of the meaning of his life is to be found in the writings of Elizabeth Hamilton, and especially in *The Desert My Dwelling Place*.[30]

Charles de Foucauld's vision was taken up by others after his death, and not least of all by René Voillaume and Little Sister Magdeleine. It is in large measure through their work that the Little Brothers and Little Sisters of Jesus have been established throughout the world. They and their successors have provided a rich variety of popular writings which serve as both a commentary upon the desert ideal as it was interpreted by de Foucauld and the desert tradition of prayer and encounter as it is being explored in so many places today.[31]

An awareness of the desert has been brought before large numbers of people through the writings of recent travellers. Geoffrey Moorhouse's book *The Fearful Void* recounts his attempt to explore in the desert the extremities of his own fear, so that he might face with confidence all the deserts of the mind with which life might confront him. He is by background and profession a journalist. He does not write from the stand-point of Christian faith; and yet he portrays not merely the hazards of travelling in the desert, but also the experience of the desert as a place of truth.[32] The vast emptiness of the desert and its capacity to humble and to illuminate are conveyed by Michael Asher's book *In Search of the Forty Days' Road*;[33] while David Praill's *Return to the Desert* traces both his journey from Mount Hermon to Mount Sinai and his encounter with the silence and the solitude of the desert.[34]

These are the aspects of desert spirituality – silence and solitude, together with unceasing prayer – that are reflected upon by Henri Nouwen and Carlo Carretto in their sensitive studies of the desert experience.[35] Something of the wisdom of the early Desert Fathers is captured by Marcel Driot[36] and Derek Webster[37]; while a significant book which deserves to be better known, *The Hermitage Within*, written by a Cistercian monk who publishes only in the name of A Monk, captures so much of the spirituality of the desert under the headings of The Desert, The Mountain, The Temple and The Cell.[38]

It is impossible to exaggerate the importance of Thomas Merton in recent decades as an expositor of the desert tradition. His vocation to be a Cistercian monk and a hermit provides the backcloth to a succession of writings which provide mature and tested reflections upon the life of solitude.[39] But Merton penetrated the desert tradition of *solitude* and *encounter*. His preoccupation in the later years of his life with the conflicts of contemporary political and social issues ensured that his particular kind of desert spirituality remained fundamentally world-affirming.[40]

Solitude, testing, self-emptying, encounter and transfiguration: these are the five themes that encapsulate the story and the spirituality of the desert. It is not the least of the achievements of several writers in recent years that their exposition of the desert tradition has held all five in a creative tension. The solitude and the testing and the self-emptying, which are inseparable from the desert experience, must also embrace encounter and transfiguration.

It was Thomas Merton's conviction that solitude and contemplation are not to be set over against society and action. On the contrary, Christian contemplation involved for him an engagement with God so that the course of human history might be shaped according to the truth, the mercy and the faithfulness of God.[41] Alessandro Pronzato in his book *Meditations on the Sand* depicts the desert as 'an essential dimension of life'.[42] He insists that the experience of the desert takes us back to our 'former environment, work and daily life'.[43] He asks that the true disciple of the desert might enter the disturbed solitude of life,[44] and he pleads for 'oases of spirituality in our cities where there are individuals capable of waiting and hoping instead of hurrying and worrying'.[45]

There are those who believe that 'the call of the desert is being heard again',[46] that our world may be rediscovering the necessity of solitude, of waiting upon God, of contemplation. Frère Ivan writes out of the conviction that 'a contemporary religious sensibility is rediscovering the riches of a tradition it has forgotten or neglected'.[47] But it is fundamental to his argument that 'the Desert and the City are the settings for one and the same struggle', which is nothing less than a reversal of the tragedy of the human condition by its transfiguration in the power of God.[48]

NOTES

THE STORY OF THE DESERT

1. St Antony, c.251–356.
2. St Pachomius, c.290–346
3. St Ammon, obit. c.350.
4. St Macarius, c.300–390.
5. St Basil the Great, c.330–379.
6. Rufinus, c.345–410.
7. St Melania, c.383–438.
8. St Jerome, c.342–420.
9. St Palladius, c.365–425.
10. John Cassian, c.360–435.
11. St Athanasius, c.296–373.
12. Cited by Anson, Peter, *The Call of the Desert*, SPCK 1964, p. 15.
13. Louth, Andrew, *The Wilderness of God*, Darton, Longman and Todd 1991, p. 62.
14. *Historia Monachorum in Aegypto*, Trans. by Russell, Norman; Introduction by Ward, Benedicta; Mowbray 1980, p. 3.
15. *Historia Monachorum in Aegypto*.
16. St Benedict, c.480–550.
17. St Romauld, c.952–1027.
18. St Bruno, c.1032–1101.
19. St Bernard of Clairvaux, 1090–1150.
20. Colossians 3.3.
21. Julian of Norwich, c.1342–post 1413.
22. Louth, Andrew, *op. cit.*, p.80.
23. Leclercq, Jean, *Alone with God*, Preface by Merton, Thomas, Hodder and Stoughton 1961, p.14.
24. Leech, Kenneth, *True God*, Sheldon Press 1985, p. 150.
25. St John of the Cross, 1542–1591.
26. Charles de Foucauld, 1858–1916.
27. *Letter*, Abbé Huvelin to Charles de Foucauld, 9th December 1897. Cited by Louth, Andrew, *op. cit.*, p. 10.
28. Cited by Louth, Andrew, *op. cit.*, p. 13.
29. de Foucauld, Charles, *Letters from the Desert*, Burns & Oates 1977, p. 83.
30. St John 12. 24–31.
31. de Foucauld, Charles, *op. cit.*, p. 143.
32. Eliot, T.S., *The Waste Land*.
33. Merton, Thomas, *The New Man*, Burns & Oates 1961, pp. 2–3.
34. Solzhenitsyn, Alexander, *Gulag Archipelago*.
35. Thomas, R.S., *Collected Poems 1945–1990*, J.M. Dent 1993.
36. Leech, Kenneth, *op. cit.*, 154.
37. Isaiah 35. 1–7.

THE SPIRITUALITY OF THE DESERT

1. Asher, Michael, *In Search of the Forty Days' Road*, London 1984. Cited by Prail, David, *Return to the Desert*, Fount 1995, p. 187.

2. Serge Boulgakov. Cited by Monk, A, *The Hermitage Within*, Trans. by Neame, Alan, Darton, Longman and Todd 1977, p. 6.
3. Ward, Benedicta, Introduction to *Historia Monachorum in Aegypto*, Trans. by Russell, Norman, Mowbray 1980, p. 34.
4. Hannay, James O., *The Wisdom of the Desert*, Methuen & Co. 1904, p. 24.
5. Monk, A., *op. cit.*, p. 14.
6. Colossians 3.3.
7. Cassian, John, *Conferences* II.4. Cited by Driot, Marcel, *Fathers of the Desert*, St Paul's Publications 1992, p. 52.
8. St Matthew 5.6.
9. Abbot Moses, Cited by Waddell, Helen, *The Desert Fathers*, Constable & Co 1994, p. 94.
10. Theophan the Recluse. Cited by Ware, Timothy (Editor), *The Art of Prayer: An Orthodox Anthology*, Compiled by Igumen Chariton of Valamo, Trans. by Kadloubovsky, E., and Palmer, E.M., Faber & Faber 1966, p. 73.
11. Nouwen Henri J.M., *The Way of the Heart*, Daybreak: Darton, Longman & Todd 1992, p. 69.
12. Merton, Thomas, *Seeds of Contemplation*, New York: Dell 1949. Cited by King, Thomas M., *Merton, Mystic at the Center of America*, The Liturgical Press, Collegeville, Minnesota 1992, p. 110.
13. Merton, Thomas, *Thoughts in Solitude*, Burns & Oates 1958, p. 18.
14. Monk, A., *op. cit.*, p. 66.
15. Pronzato, Alessandro, *Meditations on the Sand*, St Paul's Publications 1982, p. 83.
16. Monk, A., *op. cit.*, p. 12.
17. Abbot Pastor, Cited by Merton, Thomas, *The Wisdom of the Desert*, Sheldon Press 1974, p. 57.
18. St Matthew, 26.39b.
19. Merton, Thomas, Cited by King, Thomas M., *Merton: Mystic at the Center of America*, The Liturgical Press, Collegeville, Minnesota 1992, p. 144.
20. Charles de Foucauld. Cited by Hamilton, Elizabeth, *The Desert My Dwelling Place: A Study of Charles de Foucauld 1858–1916*, Hodder & Stoughton 1968, p. 189.
21. St Ignatius. Cited by Carretto, Carlo, *Letters from the Desert*, Darton, Longman and Todd 1972, p. 19.
22. Cited by Monk, A., *op. cit.*, p. 141.
23. Nouwen, Henri J.-M., *op. cit.*, p. 64.
24. Ward, Benedicta, Introduction to *Historia Monachorum in Aegypto*, *op. cit.*, p. 35.
25. St Antony. Cited by Louth, Andrew, *op. cit.*, p. 59.
26. Hamilton, Elizabeth, *op. cit.*, p. 218.
27. Pronzato, Alessandro, *op. cit.*, p. 103.
28. *Ibid.* p. 99.
29. Maritain, Jacques and Raissa, *Liturgy and Contemplation*.
30. Monk, A., *op. cit.*, p. 141.
31. Carretto, Carlo, *op. cit.*, pp. 134–5.

32. St Irenaeus, *Against Heresies*, I.6.2.
33. Webster, Derek *The Abbott and the Dwarf*, St Paul's Publications 1992, p. 83.
34. Ward, Benedicta, *Introduction* to *Historia Monachorum in Aegypto*, *op. cit.*, p. 34.
35 St John 17.19.
36. Seraphim of Sarov, 1759–1833.
37. Cited by Ivan, Frère, *Desert and the City*, Trans. by Orbell, Rachel, St Paul's Publications 1993, p. 8.
38. Isaiah 51. 7.
39. Romans 8. 19–21.

AN ANTHOLOGY FOR LENT

ASH WEDNESDAY: THE CALL OF THE DESERT

ASH WEDNESDAY

1. Pronzato, Alessandro, *op. cit.*, p. 45.
2. *Ibid.* p. 3.
3. Hamilton, Elizabeth, *op. cit.*, p. 229.
4. Monk, A., *op. cit.*, p. 12.
5. Webster, Derek, *op. cit.*, p. 104.
6. Monk, A., *op. cit.*, p. 18.
7. Webster, Derek, *Sands of Silence*, St Paul's Publications 1993, p. 58.

THURSDAY

1. Moorhouse, Geoffrey, *The Fearful Void*, Paladin Books 1975, pp. 127–8.
2. Ivan, Frère, *op. cit.*, p. 99.
3. Monk, A., *op. cit.*, p. 13.
4. *Ibid.*, p. 7.
5. *Ibid.*, p. 94.

FRIDAY

1. Pronzato, Alessandro, *op. cit.*, pp. 2–3.
2. *Ibid.*, pp. 1–2.

SATURDAY

1. Carretto, Carlo, *op. cit.*, p. 35.
2. Monk, A., *op. cit.*, p. 92.
3. Pronzato, Alessandro, *op. cit.*, pp. 4–5.
4. Prail, David, *op. cit.*, p. 184.
5. Webster, Derek, *Sounds of Silence*, St Paul's Publications 1993, p. 114.

FIRST SUNDAY IN LENT: SOLITUDE

SUNDAY

1. Anson, Peter F., *The Call of the Desert*, SPCK 1964, p.xvii.

2. Monk, A., *op. cit.*, p. 28.
3. Merton, Thomas, *Thoughts in Solitude*, Burns & Oates 1958, p. 93.
4. Leclercq, Jean, *Alone with God*, Hodder & Stoughton 1961, p. 27.
5. Abbot Allois, *Pelagius, xi.5*, Cited by Ware, Timothy (Editor) *op. cit.*, p. 18.
6. William of Saint-Thierry, Cited by Monk, A., *op. cit.*, p. 8.

MONDAY
1. Lerclerq, Jean, *op. cit.*, p. 77.
2. Merton, Thomas, *op. cit.*, p. 90.
3. Theophan the Recluse, cited by Ware, Timothy (Editor), *op. cit.*, p. 255.
4. Pronzato, Alessandro, *op. cit.*, p. 15.
5. Merton, Thomas, *op. cit.*, p. 94.

TUESDAY
1. Theophan the Recluse, Cited by Ware, Timothy (Editor), *op. cit.*, p. 187.
2. Theophan the Recluse, Cited by Ware, Timothy (Editor), *op. cit.*, p. 254.
3. Merton, Thomas, *op. cit.*, p. 81.

WEDNESDAY
1. Pronzato, Alessandro, *op. cit.*, p. 89.
2. Leclercq, Jean, *op. cit.*, p. 79.
3. *Ibid.*
4. Foucauld, Charles de, *op. cit.*, p. 84.
5. Ivan, Frère, *op. cit.*, p. 68.
6. St John of the Cross, Maxim 147, Cited by Monk, A., *op. cit.*, p. 15.

THURSDAY
1. Eliot, T.S., *East Coker. The Complete Poems and Plays*, Faber & Faber 1969.
2. Carretto, Carlo, *op. cit.*, p. xv.
3. Jerusalem Community. *Rule of Life*.
4. Soeur Marie, *Ligne de Force de Bethlehem*, Cited by Pronzato, Alessandro, *op. cit.*, p. 17.

FRIDAY
1. Merton, Thomas, *Preface*, Leclercq, Jean, *op. cit.*, p. 15.
2. Merton, Thomas, Cited by Stone, Naomi Burton and Hart, Patrick, *Love and Living*, New York: Bantam 1980, p. 15.
3. Pronzato, Alessandro, *op. cit.*, p. 16.
4. Merton, Thomas, *Seeds of Contemplation*, New York: Dell 1949. Cited by King, Thomas M., *Merton, Mystic at the Center of America*, The Liturgical Press, Collegeville, Minnesota 1992, p. 110.
5. Brother Daniel-Ange, Cited by Pronzato, Alessandro, *op. cit.*, p. 16.
6. Pronzato, Alessandro, *op. cit.*, p. 18.

7. Merton, Thomas, *Raids on the Unspeakable*, Burns & Oates, 1977, p. 20.
8. Carretto, Carlo, *op. cit.*, p. xx.

SATURDAY
1. Merton, Thomas, *Raids on the Unspeakable*, Burns & Oates 1977, p. 20.
2. Pascal, Blaise, *Penseés, No. 136*, Trans by Krailsheimer, Harmondsworth 1966, p. 67.
3. Merton, Thomas, *Thoughts in Solitude*, Burns & Oates 1958, p. 97.
4. *Ibid.*, p. 12.
5. *Ibid.*, pp. 12–13.
6. Merton, Thomas.
7. Merton, Thomas, *Raids on the Unspeakable*, Burns & Oates 1977, p. 20, but drawing also upon Ionesco, Eugène, *Rhinoceros.*

SECOND SUNDAY IN LENT

SUNDAY
1. Monk, A., *op. cit.*, p. 26.
2. Ivan, Frére, *op. cit.*, p. 90.
3. Monk, A., *op. cit.*, p. 66.
4. *Ibid.*, p. 81.
5. Pronzato, Alessandro, *op. cit.*, p. 47.
6. A Desert Father, Cited by Driot, Marcel, *Fathers of the Desert*, St Paul's Publications, 1992, p. 68.

MONDAY
1. Merton, Thomas, *Preface*, Leclercq, Jean, *op. cit.*, p. 16.
2. Louth, Andrew, *op. cit.*, p. 51.
3. Merton, Thomas, *Thoughts in Solitude*, Burns & Oates 1958, p. 18.
4. Ivan, Frère, *op. cit.*, p. 92.
5. Prail, David *op. cit.*, p. 184.
6. Monk, A., *op. cit.*, p. 14.

TUESDAY
1. A Desert Father, Cited by Merton, Thomas, *The Wisdom of the Desert*, Sheldon Press 1974, p. 73.
2. Abbot Sisoes, Trans. and Cited by Ward, Benedicta, *The Sayings of the Desert Fathers*, Mowbray 1975, p. 185.
3. A Desert Father, Cited by Ward, Benedicta, *The Wisdom of the Desert Fathers*, Sisters of the Love of God Press 1991, p. 40.
4. Pronzato, Alessandro, *op. cit.*, p. 83.
5. Webster, Derek, *The Abbot and the Dwarf*, St Paul's Publications 1992, p. 78.

WEDNESDAY
1. Cited by Driot, Marcel, *op. cit.*, p. 24.
2. Merton, Thomas, *Thoughts in Solitude*, Burns & Oates 1958, p. 48.

3. Abbot Pastor, Cited by Merton, Thomas, *The Wisdom of the Desert*, Sheldon Press 1974, p. 62.
4. Theophan the Recluse, Cited by Ware, Timothy (Editor), p. 271.
5. Abbot Pastor, Cited by Merton, Thomas, *The Wisdom of the Desert*, Sheldon Press 1974, p. 57.

THURSDAY
1. Pronzato, Alessandro, *op. cit.*, p. 7.
2. Driot, Marcel, *op. cit.*, p. 17.

FRIDAY
1. A Desert Father, Cited by Ward, Benedicta, *The Wisdom of the Desert Fathers*, Sisters of the Love of God Press 1991, p. 9.
2. A Desert Father, Cited by Merton, Thomas, *The Wisdom of the Desert*, Sheldon Press 1974, p. 45.
3. Chardin, Teilhard de.

SATURDAY
1. Merton, Thomas, *Raids on the Unspeakable*, Burns & Oates 1977, p. 16.
2. Brother Roger of Taizé.
3. Theophan the Recluse, Cited by Ware, Timothy (Editor), p. 231.
4. Merton, Thomas, *Thoughts in Solitude*, Burns & Oates 1958, p. 24.
5. A Desert Father. Cited by Ward, Benedicta, *The Wisdom of the Desert Fathers*, Sisters of the Love of God Press 1991, p. 40.

THIRD SUNDAY IN LENT: SELF-EMPTYING

SUNDAY
1. Carretto, Carlo, *In Search of the Beyond*, Darton, Longman & Todd, 1975, p. 167.
2. Webster, Derek, *Sands of Silence*, St Paul's Publications 1993, p. 95.
3. Attributed to Anthony, Deacon of the Church in Ephesus. Cited by Webster, Derek, *Sands of Silence*, St Paul's Publications 1993, p. 102.
4. Merton, Thomas, *Thoughts in Solitude*, Burns & Oates 1958, p. 70.

MONDAY
1. Abbot Alonius. Cited by Merton, Thomas, *The Wisdom of the Desert*, Sheldon Press 1974, p. 53.
2. Theophan the Recluse, Cited by Ware, Timothy (Editor), *op. cit.*, p. 187.
3. The Desert Fathers. Cited by Ware, Timothy (Editor), *op. cit.*, p. 150.
4. Abbot Sisois. Cited by Ware, Timothy (Editor), *op. cit.*, pp. 168–9.
5. Abbess Syncletica. Cited by Ward, Benedicta, *The Sayings of the Desert Fathers*, Mowbray 1975, p. 197.

TUESDAY
1. St John of the Cross, *Ascent of Mount Carmel* i, xiii.

2. Abbot Pastor. Cited by Ware, Timothy (Editor), *op. cit.*, p. 144.
3. Merton, Thomas, *Contemplative Prayer*, Darton, Longman & Todd 1975, p. 84.
4. St Teresa of Avila. Found in St Teresa's breviary after her death. Cited by Hamilton, Elizabeth, *The Servants of Love: The Spirituality of Teresa of Avila*, Darton, Longman & Todd 1975 p. 103.

WEDNESDAY
1. Charles de Foucauld. Cited by Hamilton, Elizabeth, *op. cit.*, p. 189.
2. Charles de Foucauld, *Ibid.*, p. 189.
3. Abbot Moses. Cited by Hannay, James O., *The Wisdom of the Desert*, Methuen & Co. 1904, p. 88.
4. Pronzato, Alessandro, *op. cit.*, p. 71.
5. Merton, Thomas, *Seeds of Contemplation*, Burns & Oates 1960, p. 24.

THURSDAY
1. *Way of Perfection* xxiii.
2. Ivan, Frère, *op. cit.*, p. 116.
3. Merton, Thomas, *Thoughts in Solitude*, Burns & Oates 1958, p. 31.
4. Voillaume, René, *Seeds of the Desert*, Anthony Clarke Books, Wheathampstead, Hertfordshire 1972, p. 66.
5. St Ignatius. Cited by Carretto, Carlo, *Letters from the Desert*, Darton, Longman & Todd 1972, p. 19.
6. Merton, Thomas, *The Power and Meaning of Love*, Sheldon Press, 1976, p. 68.
7. The Jesus Prayer in the Orthodox Church. Cited by Ware, Timothy (Editor), *op. cit.*, p. 9.

FRIDAY
1. Merton, Thomas, *Seeds of Contemplation*, Burns & Oates 1960, p. 46.
2. Thomas, R.S., *Via Negativa*.
3. Merton, Thomas.
4. Pronzato, Alessandro, *op. cit.*, p. 80.
5. Merton, Thomas, *No Man Is An Island*, Burns & Oates 1985, p. 209.

SATURDAY
1. Pronzato, Alessandro, *op. cit.*, p. 19.
2. Merton, Thomas, *Thoughts in Solitude*, Burns & Oates 1958, p. 27.
3. Voillaume, René, *op. cit.*, p. 72.
4. Cassian, *Collationes* x.7. Cited by Ware, Timothy (Editor), *op. cit.*, p. 27.
5. Merton, Thomas. Cited by King, Thomas M., *op. cit.*, p. 144.
6. Foucauld, Charles de. Cited by Carretto, Carlo, *In Search of the Beyond*, Darton Longman and Todd 1975, p. 107.

FOURTH SUNDAY IN LENT: ENCOUNTER

SUNDAY
1. St Augustine of Hippo. Cited by Driot, Marcel, *op. cit.*, p. 125.
2. Abbot Nicholas. Cited by Webster, Derek, *Sands of Silence*, St Paul's Publications 1993, p. 55.
3. Pronzato, Alessandro, *op. cit.*, p. 60.
4. *Ibid.*, pp. 103–4.
5. A Desert Father. Cited by Ward, Benedicta, *The Wisdom of the Desert Fathers*, Sisters of the Love of God Press 1991, p. 34.
6. St Bernard of Clairvaux. Cited by Merton, Thomas, *The Power and the Meaning of Love*, Sheldon Press 1976, p. 110.

MONDAY
1. Carretto, Carlo, *In Search of the Beyond*, Darton Longman and Todd, 1975, p. 14.
2. St Augustine of Hippo, *Soliloquies*, Cited by Louth, Andrew, *op. cit.*, p. 74.
3. Merton, Thomas, Cited by Hart, Patrick (Editor), *The Monastic Journey*, Garden City: Image Books 1978, p. 223.
4. Abbot Souros. *Historia Monachorum in Aegypto*, Trans. by Russell, Norman, Mowbray 1980, p. 88.
5. Merton, Thomas, *Seeds of Contemplation*, Burns & Oates 1960, p. 108.

TUESDAY
1. Carretto, Carlo, *In Search of the Beyond*, Darton Longman and Todd 1975, p. 62.
2. St Thomas à Kempis, *The Imitation of Christ*, ii.8.
3. *St Patrick's Breastplate*. According to St Patrick. Trans. by Mrs C.F. Alexander.
4. Charles de Foucauld. Cited by Carretto, Carlo, *Letters from the Desert*, Darton Longman and Todd 1972, p. 97.
5. Charles de Foucauld. Cited by Voillaume, René, op. cit., *p. 56.*

WEDNESDAY
1. Merton, Thomas, *Thoughts in Solitude*, Burns & Oates 1958, p. 21.
2. Merton, Thomas, *Seeds of Contemplation*, Burns & Oates 1960, p. 11.
3. Isaac the Syrian. Cited by Nouwen, Henri J.M., *The Way of the Heart*, Daybreak: Darton Longman and Todd 1992, p. 78.
4. Merton, Thomas, *Seeds of Contemplation*, Burns & Oates 1960, p. 13.
5. Merton, Thomas, *Seeds of Contemplation*, New York: Dell 1949, pp. 139–140. Cited by King, Thomas, M., *op. cit.*, p. 48.

THURSDAY
1. Merton, Thomas, *Seeds of Contemplation*, Burns & Oates 1960, p. 20.

2. Carretto, Carlo, *In Search of the Beyond*, Darton Longman & Todd 1975, p. 19.
3. John the Dwarf. Cited by Louth, Andrew, *op. cit.*, p. 59.
4. St Antony. Cited by Louth, Andrew, *op. cit.*, p. 59.
5. Edwards, Edward, *Beyond the Last Oasis*, London 1985.
6. Foucauld, Charles de. Cited by Hamilton, Elizabeth *op. cit.*, p. 217.

FRIDAY
1. Merton, Thomas.
2. Merton, Thomas, *Raids on the Unspeakable*, Burns & Oates 1977, p. 16.
3. Maritain, Jacques and Raissa, *Liturgy and Contemplation*. Cited by Voillaume, René, *op. cit.*, p. 67.
4. Pronzato Alessandro, *op. cit.*, pp. 98–9.
5. Charles de Foucauld. Cited by Hamilton, Elizabeth, *op. cit.*, p. 13.
6. Monk, A., *op. cit.*, p. 141.

SATURDAY
1. Voillaume, René, *Faith and Contemplation*, Darton Longman and Todd 1974, p. 35.
2. Pronzato, Alessandro, *op. cit.*, p. 43.
3. Mother Mary Clare SLG.
4. Theophan the Recluse. Cited by Ware, Timothy (Editor), *op. cit.*, p. 51.

FIFTH SUNDAY IN LENT: TRANSFIGURATION

SUNDAY
1. Carretto, Carlo, *In Search of the Beyond*, Darton Longman & Todd, 1975, p. 17.
2. St John Chrysostom, *In Matthaei Evangelium* 39:4, P.G. 57:438.
3. Teilhard de Chardin.
4. Webster, Derek, *Sands of Silence*, St Paul's Publications 1993, p. 90.
5. Dom Helder Camara.

MONDAY
1. Merton, Thomas, *New Seeds of Contemplation*, New York: New Directions 1962, p. 207.
2. Monk, A., *op. cit.*, p. 47.
3. Leclercq, Jean, *op. cit.*, pp. 166–7.
4. Carretto, Carlo, *Letters from the Desert*, Darton Longman and Todd 1972, p. 9.
5. St Bernard of Clairvaux. Cited by Leclercq, Jean, *op. cit.*, p. 169.
6. Leclercq, Jean, *op. cit.*, p. 166.

TUESDAY
1. Brother Roger of Taizé.
2. Susan Fisher.

3. Thomas, R.S., *The Flower: Collected Poems, 1945–1990,* J.M. Dent 1993.

WEDNESDAY
1. Abbot Nicholas. Cited by Webster, Derek, *Sands of Silence,* St Paul's Publications 1993, p. 25.
2. Carretto, Carlo, *Letters from the Desert,* Darton Longman and Todd 1972, pp. 134–5.
3. Merton, Thomas, *Thoughts in Solitude,* Burns & Oates 1958, p. 25.
4. Abbot Sisoes. Cited by Ward, Benedicta, *The Sayings of the Desert Fathers,* Mowbray 1981, p. 215.
5. Abbot Joseph of Panephysis. Cited by Merton, Thomas, *The Wisdom of the Desert,* Sheldon Press 1974, p. 50.
6. St Irenaeus, *Against Heresies,* I.6.2.

THURSDAY
1. St Pachomius, Cited by *Historia Monachorum in Aegypto,* Trans. by Russell, Norman, Mowbray 1980, p. 45.
2. Merton, Thomas, *Seeds of Contemplation,* Burns & Oates 1960, p. 5.
3. Ivan, Frère, *op. cit.,* p. 19.
4. Merton, Thomas, *Seeds of Contemplation,* Burns & Oates 1960, p. 6.

FRIDAY
1. Webster, Derek, *The Abbott and the Dwarf,* St Paul's Publications 1992, pp. 82–3.

SATURDAY
1. Merton, Thomas, *The New Man,* Burns & Oates 1985, p. 34.
2. Merton, Thomas, *No Man Is An Island,* Burns & Oates 1985, p. 223.

HOLY WEEK AND EASTER DAY: THE DIVINE MYSTERY

PALM SUNDAY
1. St Luke 9.51.
2. Barth, Karl, *Dogmatics in Outline,* SCM Press 1949, p. 39.
3. Vanstone, W.H., *The Stature of Waiting,* DLT 1982, pp. 85–6.
4. Thomas, R.S., *The Coming; op. cit.*

MONDAY IN HOLY WEEK
1. St Luke 19.41–2.
2. Theophan the Recluse. Cited by Ware, Timothy (Editor), *op. cit.,* p. 231.
3. Monk, A., *op. cit.,* p. 84.
4. *Ibid.,* p. 83.

TUESDAY IN HOLY WEEK
1. St John 12. 24.
2. Monk, A., *op. cit.,* p. 81.

3. St Thomas à Kempis, *The Imitation of Christ*, iii.56.
4. St Bernard of Clairvaux, *Sermon I on St Andrew's Day*.

WEDNESDAY IN HOLY WEEK
1. St Luke 12. 49–50.
2. Merton, Thomas, *No Man Is An Island*, Burns & Oates 1985, p. 124.
3. St Ignatius of Antioch, *To the Ephesians*, 19.1.
4. Luther, Martin, *Luther's Works*, Weimar, Ausgabe V. 179.131.

MAUNDY THURSDAY
1. St Matthew 26. 39b.
2. St John of the Cross, *The Ascent of Mount Carmel*, Stanzas 3 and 4.
3. Monchanin, Abbé, Ecrits Spirituels, 126. Cited by Merton, Thomas, *Contemplative Prayer*, DLT 1975, p. 133.
4. *Um Mitternacht*, A song written by Mahler to the words of Friedrich Ruckert.

GOOD FRIDAY
1. St John 12.27–29a.
2. Romans 5.8.
3. St Mark 15.34.
4. St John 19.30.
5. St John 12.31–2.
6. Vanstone, W.H., *Love's Endeavour, Love's Expense*, DLT 1979, pp. 119–120.

EASTER EVE
1. Colossians 3.3.
2. Boros, Ladislaus, *The Cosmic Christ*, Trans, by Smith, David, Seurde Press 1975, pp. 52–3.
3. Merton, Thomas, *The New Man*, Burns & Oates 1985, pp. 2–3.
4. Webster, Derek, *The Abbot and the Dwarf*, St Paul's Publications 1992, pp. 62–3.

EASTER DAY
1. Galatians 2.20.
2. St Leo the Great, *Serm.* 64.3. Cited by Franks, R.S., *The Work of Christ*, Thos. Nelson & Sons Ltd 1962. p. 105.
3. Webster, Derek, *The Abbot and the Dwarf*, St Paul's Publications 1992, p. 108.
4. Farrer, Austin, *The End of Man*, SPCK 1973, p. 4.
5. Merton, Thomas, *Contemplative Prayer*, DLT 1975, p. 29.

THE LITERATURE OF THE DESERT

1. Hannay, James O., *The Wisdom of the Desert*, Methuen & Co., 1904.
2. Waddell, Helen, *The Desert Fathers*, Constable & Co., 1994.
3. Merton, Thomas, *The Wisdom of the Desert*, Sheldon Press 1974.

4. Ward, Benedicta, *The Sayings of the Desert Fathers*, Mowbray 1981; *The Wisdom of the Desert Fathers*, Sisters of the Love of God Press 1991.

5. St Antony, c.351–356. *The Life of St Antony* (Vita Antonii), written by St Athanasius and translated into Latin by Evagrius of Antioch, has greatly informed our understanding of early monasticism.

6. St Paul of Thebes, obit. c.340. *The Life of St Paul of Thebes (Vita Pauli)*, written by St Jerome, is a curious tissue of fact and fantasy.

7. St Pachomius, c.290–340. *The Life (or Lives) of St Pachomius, (Vita Pachomii)* presents in its various editions a mixture of fact and legend.

8. *The Sayings of the Fathers*. Originally known as the *Apophthegmata Patrum*, they were translated from Greek to Latin by Pelagius and took the more familiar title of the *Verba Seniorum*.

9. *The Lausiac History*, written by Palladius c.419, has been judged to be the most important work regarding the early history of monasticism.

10. *Historia Monachorum in Aegypto*. Authorship unknown. Translated from the Greek text by Rufinus of Aquileia. See *Historia Monachorum in Aegypto, (The Lives of the Desert Fathers)*, Trans. by Russell, Norman, Mowbray 1980.

11. The *Conferences* of John Cassian were based in large measure on conversations between the author and the Desert Fathers.

12. The *Institutes* of John Cassian lay down the basic rules for the ordering of the monastic life. Their primary concern is the community life of the monastery and, drawing upon the experience of the Egyptian hermits, they discuss the eight principal stumbling blocks to perfection.

13. The *Rule of St Pachomius* survives in a Latin translation by Jerome, although fragments of the *Rule* survive in Greek and Coptic.

14. St Benedict of Nursia, c.480–c.550.

15. The *Rule of St Benedict* was compiled to order the common life of the monks. Much of the *Rule* is drawn from the earlier *Rules* of Basil the Great, John Cassian and Caesarius of Arles.

16. Lossky, Vladimir, *The Mystical Theology of the Eastern Church*, James Clarke & Co. 1957.

17. *The Art of Prayer: An Orthodox Anthology*, Compiled by Igumen Chariton; Trans. by E. Kadloubovsky and E.M. Palmer; Edited with an Introduction by Timothy Ware; Faber & Faber 1966.

18. *Ibid*, p. 10.

19. Anson, Peter F., *The Call of the Desert*, SPCK 1964.

20. Leclercq, Jean, *Alone with God*, Trans. by McCabe, Elizabeth, Hodder and Stoughton 1961.

21. *Ibid*. From the Preface by Merton, Thomas, p. 12.

22. The original form of Giustiniani's *Rule* was written in 1516. This was followed by the *Regula vitae eremiticae* in 1520. *The Constitutions for the Company of Hermits of St Romauld* were drawn up in 1524.

23. Leclercq, Jean, *op. cit.*, p. 27.

24. Thomas Merton's *Notes for a Philosophy of Solitude* are to be found

in his book *The Power and Meaning of Love*, Sheldon Press 1976. pp. 43–73.

25. St John of the Cross, *Collected Poems and Writings*.
26. T.S. Eliot, *The Complete Poems and Plays*, Faber and Faber 1987.
27. R.S. Thomas, *Collected Poems 1945–1990*, J.M. Dent 1993.
28. Louth, Andrew, *op. cit.*
29. de Foucauld, Charles, *Letters from the Desert*, Burns & Oates 1977.
30. Hamilton, Elizabeth, *The Desert My Dwelling Place: A Study of Charles de Foucauld 1858–1916*, Hodder and Stoughton 1968.
31. Voillaume, René, *Seeds of the Desert*, Anthony Clarke Books 1972; *Faith and Contemplation*, Darton, Longman & Todd 1974; *Christian Vocation*, London 1973; *Religious Life in Today's World*, Ottawa 1970. Spink, Kathryn, *The Call of the Desert: A Biography of Little Sister Magdeleine of Jesus*, Darton, Longman & Todd 1993; Carretto, Carlo, *Letters from the Desert*, Darton, Longman & Todd 1972; *In Search of the Beyond*, Darton, Longman & Todd, 1975; *Summoned by Love*, Darton, Longman & Todd 1977; *The Desert in the City*, Fount Paperbacks 1983.
32. Moorhouse, Geoffrey, *The Fearful Void*, Paladin Books 1975.
33. Asher, Michael, *In Search of the Forty Days' Road*, London 1984.
34. Praill, David, *Return to the Desert*, Fount 1995.
35. Nouwen, Henri J.M., *The Way of the Heart*, Daybreak: Darton, Longman & Todd 1992. Carretto, Carlo, see *Letters from the Desert* (note 31 above).
36. Driot, Marcel, *Fathers of the Desert*, St Paul's Publications 1992.
37. Webster, Derek, *The Abbot and the Dwarf*, St Paul's Publications 1992; *Sands of Silence*, St Paul's Publications 1993; *Bread for a Wilderness*, St Paul's Publications 1995.
38. Monk, A., *The Hermitage Within*, Trans. by Neame, Alan, Darton, Longman & Todd, 1977.
39. Merton, Thomas, *The Waters of Silence*, Hollis & Carter 1954; *The Silent Life*, Burns & Oates 1957; *Thoughts in Solitude*, Burns & Oates 1958; *Seeds of Contemplation*, Burns & Oates 1960; *The Power and Meaning of Love*, Sheldon Press 1976.
40. Merton, Thomas, *Raids on the Unspeakable*, Burns & Oates 1993. King, Thomas, M., *Merton: Mystic at the Center of America*. The Liturgical Press, Collegeville, Minnesota 1992.
41. Merton, Thomas, *Spiritual Direction and Meditation*. The Liturgical Press, Collegeville, Minnesota 1962.
42. Pronzato, Alessandro, *op. cit.*
43. *Ibid.*, p. 47.
44. *Ibid.*, pp. 98–9.
45. *Ibid.*, pp. 103–4.
46. Anson, Peter F., *op. cit.*, p. xvi.
47. Ivan, Frère, *The Desert and the City*, St Paul's Publications 1993. p. 11.
48. *Ibid.*, p. 10.

CPSIA information can be obtained
at www.ICGtesting.com
Printed in the USA
FSHW021501210720
72346FS